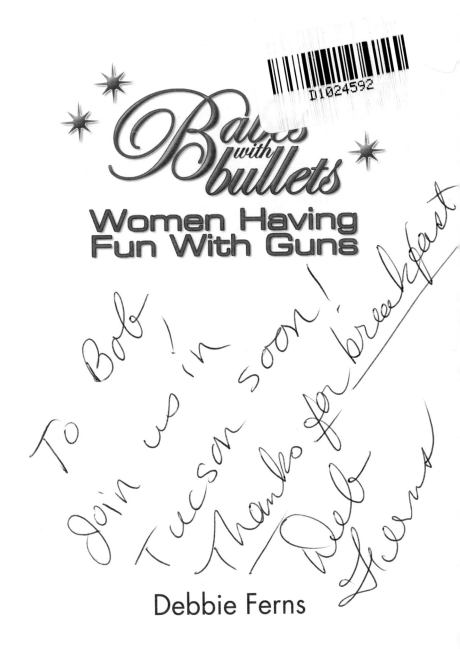

Babes with bullets

Women Having Fun With Guns

To Bob !
Join us in
Tucson soon !
Thanks for breakfast
Deb Ferns

Debbie Ferns

Women Having Fun With Guns

Debbie Ferns

Published by:
Bullseye Trading Post, LLC
7850 N. Silverbell
Suite 114-315
Tucson, AZ 85743

www.BabesWithBullets.net

Printed in the United States of America

Cover design and layout: Ad Graphics, Inc., Tulsa, OK
Editor: Sherrill J. Thayer

ISBN: 0-9763395-9-5

DEDICATION

Every woman should be so blessed as to have two great men in her life.

To my husband, Gary, your support during all my adventures over the last three decades is beyond description! I want you to know that I appreciate you and that I love you.

To my dad, Ray Mousseau, who is gone now but not forgotten. My love of sports and the outdoors came from him. He was a good man and a great dad.

SPECIAL TRIBUTES

To my family members, Robert Ian and Sherrill Thayer; a thank you isn't enough. It was your encouragement, guidance and writing knowledge that made this book possible.

My daughter, Casey Ferns, was a tremendous asset in helping me with the flow of the book. She was also very patient in teaching me new skills on the computer.

A big "You Rock" to Lisa Munson, my mentor in shooting sports. Thank you so much for traveling from Seattle to Tucson to help me polish the book.

I am very grateful to Sandy Froman, incoming president for the National Rifle Association. Thank you for sharing my enthusiasm to introduce more women to shooting sports.

The suggestions and encouragement from Julie Goloski about the book (and my ability in shooting sports) has been invaluable.

I owe a debt of gratitude to the men and women that agreed to be part of the book through interviews and information. Thanks for joining me on a fun adventure!

ACKNOWLEDGMENTS

To the other quality women in my life that make the difference between joy and despair on almost a daily basis:

My mom, Susan Mousseau, a mother hen extraordinaire

Oldest daughter, Raya Ferns, who gets me to laugh at the oddest moments

"Rowdy Rangers" Sharon Boenzi & Linda Dent, I hope the adventures continue…

NAWBO Mastermind Compatriots: Jan Aalberts, MJ Jensen, Gail Holan and Mary Darling. You are the best board of directors that an author ever had!

My patient web designer, Jeanie Darnell from Desert Creations, deserves many thanks for sticking with me through this project.

Further Acknowledgments

Bill Goloski designed the original logo for the book and has been a trooper ever since.

Thank you to the Videosyncrasy team of Bob Martin and Marilyn Vogel. They, along with director Ruby Peckford, made the book come alive with a wonderful 7 minute DVD film.

Several of the pictures in the book, including the one used for my biography, were a gift from Robert Townsend. Thank you for making me look so good!

Thank you to Greg Stutz from Tombstone Tactical. He loaned me part of his booth at SHOT show so I could introduce this book.

TABLE OF CONTENTS

. . . .

"When you are faced with a major life challenge,
ask yourself three questions:

What's the *best* that could happen?
What's the *worst* that could happen?

Now ask yourself: what is *likely* to happen?

Your answer to the last question
helps you see things *realistically*.

Now you begin to realize:

Most of the things you worry about,
never happen.

Enjoy the moment. Paradise is now."

– Robert Ian
Author, Hypnotist and Motivational Speaker
www.ReflectionsOfSuccess.com

. . . .

FOREWORD

Any woman, young or old, who has ever used a firearm to shoot at a paper or steel target, will understand why this book was written. The thrill of hitting what you are aiming at is something that I still enjoy after more than twenty years of shooting. For those of you who haven't had that experience yet, I hope this book will encourage you to try something new. You may find, as I did, that shooting sports become a part of your life and something you can't imagine giving up. Even if you don't participate every week or every month, at the very least you will learn valuable firearms safety information. This training could be important to you, and to your family, one day in the future. If you are afraid of guns then a safe and fun first-time shooting experience, like the ones described in this book, will help you conquer that fear.

As the First Vice-President of the National Rifle Association of America (NRA), I represent the Association all over the country. I attend gun safety training programs, national shooting competitions, charity events, and political meetings. It is a volunteer position and what I give up in income I gain in the opportunity to meet wonderful folks throughout America. These people, like me, care about preserving our firearms freedom. During my travels I've come to the conclusion that too many women in America think that shooting sports are just for men. They're wrong. Women like me, women interviewed in this book, women like you, are important to shooting sports and to the NRA! To give you an example, I was recently at my local salon having my nails done. A woman who had occupied the manicure station before me had moved to a nearby seat, waiting for her nails to dry. She was in her late 40's, attractive and well dressed. I began chatting with my manicurist, a long-time friend, and she asked if I had been doing any traveling for NRA lately.

When my manicurist friend mentioned "NRA," I noticed that the other woman looked over and leaned a little closer to listen to our conversation. I didn't mind her eavesdropping. I don't keep my NRA involvement a secret. In fact, like many men I see shopping at my local grocery store wearing their NRA baseball caps, I am proud that people know where I stand on the issue of freedom and firearms. Finally, the woman looked over and asked: "Do you work for the NRA?" I thought to myself: "Here we go, she probably hates guns and I'm going to hear all about it." This wasn't my first time defending the NRA so I smiled pleasantly and said: "Well, I do volunteer work for the National Rifle Association, in fact, I'm the first vice president of the Association." My manicurist chimed in: "Sandy's going to be the president of the NRA in April." The woman smiled back and said: "Wow, that's great! My husband and I are both NRA members. He's a doctor and I'm a nurse. We really enjoy shooting together." The conversation digressed into a discussion of our favorite guns and shooting sports. She shoots competitive pistol and I'm just learning sporting clays. Then we went on to talk about our non-gun hobbies, like her enthusiasm for tennis and golf, while I enjoy rubber-stamping and scrap booking. Before she left, we exchanged names and telephone numbers. I'm looking forward to calling her to get together and go shooting.

There are more opportunities for American women to get involved in the shooting sports today than ever before. There are programs specifically directed to introducing women to competitive and recreational shooting. Some are discussed in the book like NRA's "Women on Target." Other programs, like NRA's "Refuse to Be A Victim," teach women how to design their own personal protection strategy whether or not they choose to own a firearm. I'm going to suggest to my niece that she let me sponsor her for this course before she leaves home to start college.

This book also discusses other shooting programs for women offered by local ranges. One of the programs, the Annie Oakley Sure Shots, is a weekly event held at the Ben Avery Shooting Facility in Phoenix, Arizona. While at this event I met a woman who had recently been divorced and moved to Arizona. She said she had grown up afraid of guns but now that she lived in Arizona, which she thought of as the "Wild West," she had come to the Annie Oakley program for the sole purpose of getting over her fear. She never intended to buy a gun and she laughed as she said to me: "I've been coming here (Ben Avery Range) for six months. I own four guns now and have even competed in a few matches. I love shooting! I try to come to the range every week and I've brought three lady friends who shoot with me now."

These types of programs are designed for women and taught by women. The folks running these programs know how important "creature comforts" are to those of us of the fairer sex. They make sure the restroom facilities at the range are clean. The women instructors know what equipment the novice lady shooter will need to be comfortable in this new environment. Many women learn to shoot at an early age, usually taught by a father or husband, or possibly a boy-friend. But there are so many more women across American today that are unmarried, divorced or widowed, who have never touched a gun. These women are looking for professional instruction and an organized shooting program to fit their busy schedules. Everything a woman wants to know about the shooting sports is out there waiting for you. This book will guide you along the way and answer many of your questions and concerns. Give the shooting sports a try. I know that you won't be disappointed. I am confident you will find fun and friends, along with new experiences and adventures along the way.

Sandy Froman
Tucson, Arizona
November 2004

CHAPTER ONE

Why *Babes With Bullets?*

I wanted a book *devoted to women, written by a woman,* painting a picture of how or why a gal would get involved in shooting sports. The term shooting sports doesn't involve hunting events. Instead a variety of guns are used for games where each person shoots at paper, steel, clay or balloon targets. These games include a wide variety of equipment and can be played by people from every walk of life. So regardless of age, marital status, or even disabilities, there is a shooting sport for you!

I shot my first gun at the ripe middle age of 45. Over the last five years a variety of shooting sports have become my new adventures. I shared this feeling with dozens of other middle age women who also picked up a gun for the first time when they were 30, 40 or 50 years old. None of us have made the military a career, nor are we in law enforcement. So what got these gals interested in shooting sports? What kinds of experiences have they had over the years? What advice would they share with other women about participating in shooting sports?

Then I started thinking about junior shooters, who are children in an age range of 9 to 19. With the divorce rate estimated at over 50%, it stands to reason that there are a significant number of single mothers raising children alone. How are these women introducing their families to guns, to gun safety or to shooting sports? So in a way this project was borne from my desire to introduce more women and also their families to the possibility of having fun with guns.

By the Way...

When terms are used like range officer, or some other phrase that's specific to shooting sports, there is an area in the back titled "Lingo For Ladies," giving you translations. Along with the translations are the Resource pages listing web sites of gun clubs, gun organizations or associations covered in the interviews. I will continue to add information on additional shooting sports groups at the www.babeswithbullets.net site as time goes by.

The Resource pages list the National Rifle Association (NRA) but I wanted to give you more than just a web site. I think you'll enjoy getting to know Sandy Froman, the incoming NRA president. I met her as I started writing *Babes With Bullets* and her assistance has been invaluable. I think her story will surprise most of you. Sandy is 55 years old now and was raised in the San Francisco Bay Area in a "non-gun" environment. Sandy admits she probably wouldn't have considered owning a gun but when she 32 years old, and going through a divorce, she became a victim of an attempted home invasion. As Sandy stated: "I got my undergraduate degree from Stanford and my law degree from Harvard. I was working for a large L.A. law firm and never considered having a gun. Having an intruder at my door, and feeling totally helpless, was an epiphany for me." Her neighbors did not respond to her calls for help and it took the police almost 20 minutes to arrive.

Sandy Froman, First Vice-President National Rifle Association, incoming NRA President

Realizing that she alone was responsible for her own safety, Sandy went to a gun shop the following day to purchase a firearm. Fortunately the staff at the gun store encouraged her to attend a gun safety course at their indoor range. From the start Sandy was very accurate with her firearm. One of the first things she did after completing her gun safety program was to join the NRA. Like some of the other ladies that I interviewed it was through her interest in guns that she met her second husband, Bruce Nelson. Bruce was not only involved with the California Department of Justice; he was also an internationally renowned holster designer. They relocated to Tucson, Arizona, where Bruce continued with his holster business and Sandy resumed her law practice. Eventually she opened up her own law office just a few miles away from my home.

Unfortunately Bruce passed away in 1995. Sandy continued her firearms training alone while volunteering in a variety of local and national NRA programs. Over the years she has participated in several of the shooting sports that are discussed in other interviews. Recently she became involved in hunting programs as well. Sandy is proud to be the incoming president of the NRA, the oldest and largest civil rights organization in the United States.

I feel like Sandy and I are on parallel missions. We both want to get more women involved in shooting sports and the NRA. I hope you get a chance to meet her; she's a great gal!

Along the Way...

I've gathered wonderful stories about gals, from all walks of life, who have fun with guns. I think you'll enjoy reading their experiences as they enthusiastically describe the social aspects of shooting sports. These women are from all over the United States and in most cases they were looking for an interest to share with their husbands, boyfriends, dad's, or other gal pals. In my case it turned out to be something my husband and I could enjoy together as our kids were leaving home. A good friend of mine, Deb Keehart, is a great shooter and a lovely single woman. According to Deb: "Participating in a variety of shooting matches is something a single gal can do on her own." So while some of these stories relate to women who find a boyfriend or husband through the shooting sports, I encourage women to join for themselves.

CHAPTER TWO

Where I Come From, Where I'm Headed...

I've now celebrated my first half-century here on earth, though I'm not sure how that happened. I've been married a long time to a fairly patient guy; in fact our 25th anniversary was on the infamous 9/11. I come from a hard-working middle class family out of the thumb area of Michigan and have spent the last couple of decades in Tucson, Arizona. It's been a bit of a wild ride as I have always worked outside our home. That doesn't mean that all my work inside the house goes away while I'm gone during the day. I suspect that many of you share my description of leaving your home in a hurry each morning. Between work, or kids, or community activities, you circle your town for what feels like hundreds of miles each day. Then at long last you arrive back into your driveway... whew, made it again!

I actively participate in a local church and throughout the years have worn some of the hats you may wear like Girl Scout leader, softball coach, PTA board member and soccer mom. Those activities fit in with being the head taxi driver for years of basketball and swim team. We've been blessed with two wonderful girls. Like many parents I'm wondering what's in store for them in the decades to come. Over the years I've developed a motto for my girls and it goes like this: "But for the Grace of God, you could have been born women in Bangladesh." Well times are changing and while I chant the same phrase I insert other places, like Iraq. Bottom line is that I want my children to value their American freedoms and rights.

My husband (Gary) and I are part of middle-class America, not rich, not poor, just working every day to make ends meet. I keep wondering if we'll be working until we're in our 80's, or longer at the rate we're going with our kids in college. I am convinced that life is not a dress rehearsal so why not enjoy trying new things now? If someone bought you *Babes With Bullets* they are encouraging you to consider shooting sports as a potential new adventure in your life.

Trying Something New...

Like so many of you I've done my share of care-taking elderly relatives, recently helping with hospice for my dad. He was a proud former Marine, and an engineer by trade. Dad was an avid hunter, NRA member, an ardent conservationist, and a prolific reader. I know his willingness to try something different is what led him to be successful in his engineering career. It also provided him with several great hunting memories.

My parents were married for 55 years before my dad passed away from cancer on July 4th, 2004. I wondered if my mom regretted not having the chance to share with my dad either hunting or the shooting sports that he enjoyed, like skeet? As mom and I talked, it became clear that hunting wasn't available to her with a limited budget and four children at home. There was also the perception back in her day that ladies participating in gun clubs wouldn't be made welcome. That isn't the case anymore. Now women are encouraged to come out to gun ranges and participate in shooting sports. So ask yourself a question and fill in the blank: "Are shooting sports something I could share with....?"

I had that lesson in mind when our youngest daughter left for college. I was almost 45 years old. My husband and I had wrapped most of our married life around our children, extended families, community activities, our home and our jobs. I didn't feel my husband and I did anything fun together anymore. We don't dance (what I really mean is that he doesn't dance), we don't agree on what cultural events to attend and usually we don't like the same types of movies. I've always had horses, along with one very noisy beloved burro named Lola. I dote on my Sebastian, who is a 205-pound Old English Mastiff. To complete the picture you have to know that my husband is allergic to the horses and not at all fond of Lola's ear shattering bray, though it does guarantee that she gets fed first! The only thing Gary says about Sebastian is that I love the dog more than him. This isn't true but I'll never convince him so I've stopped trying. Gary loves to fly small airplanes; I throw up in anything smaller than a 100-seat jet. We both love to go fishing, although I'm the one who loves water sports of all kinds. My husband claims I tried to kill him on a recent white water rafting experience. This is also not true; his life insurance policy is not nearly big enough to make that an option.

For years my husband enjoyed long-range high power rifle shooting matches. Like most shooting sports, you need to be a participant if you don't want to be bored. Since that time I've talked with a number of gals who love this type of shooting sport, but the key is that they are participating! My husband likes to hunt; I don't. I'll only get involved in tennis or golf if I can drive the refreshment cart. (I have discovered that when you're in charge of the refreshments you're the most popular person at the event.) I've tried different things, including skydiving. Some events or sports I would do again, and some I wouldn't, but at least I've tried them. I like to say that I have eclectic tastes; my husband says I'm just crazy. By now I can hope that you are getting the drift that we were struggling to find something to enjoy together since our girls were leaving the nest.

Narrowing Down the Options...

I started a daily log and for about three months I wrote down all the things I thought might work for us. I gathered ideas from magazines, reality television shows, and radio programs. If the idea sounded interesting, I put it down. For instance I saw a magazine article about horse mounted shooting done in cowboy action/fashion style. I love riding and I like the cowboy fashion stuff. So off we went to watch a mounted shooting match about one hour from our home in Tucson. I should have remembered that my husband is allergic to horses. Besides hating to ride my husband acts like dressing up in any kind of costume is a painful death for him. Over the next few months we went to watch a variety of other shooting competitions held in Arizona.

One of the events we watched was called International Defense Pistol Association (IDPA). Even though it's a game, the underlying theme relates to self-defense. Since the pace of IDPA is fairly slow I decided to try it as my first shooting sport. Just before my 45th birthday I visited a number of gun stores to find the right firearm. I have to admit I wondered if the store staff would be patient with this complete novice. Would I be talked into a purchase that wasn't right for me? Much to my relief, no one tried to sell me on any one particular gun. The staff at each location encouraged me to concentrate on how the gun felt in my hand. After the first few stores it started feeling like a shopping excursion, not that much different then finding a great pair of jeans. I always have to try on several different styles of jeans before picking the pair I think fits me the best. Over the next few weeks I tried on about a dozen semi-automatic pistols, plus several revolvers.

On my birthday my husband went with me to purchase my first gun, a 9 mm semi-automatic pistol. I received a free safety course and shooting lessons from Liz Maddy, the gun store manager. She was a big asset in making me feel comfortable with my new gun and encouraged me to compete at a local IDPA match. So off I went with my husband to participate in my very first shooting sport. I had a new gun, new holster, along with new hearing and eye protection that fit me. Overall I felt I was looking pretty spiffy.

The morning of my first match I got up to the starting line after we had already been coached on match rules and safety issues. A patient Range Officer (RO) went through the safety rules again. Then he gave me hints on how to shoot the course. He also showed me how the timer would buzz next to my ear as a signal to start on the course. Well, the timer went off and I was very quick to get my pistol out of my holster and held out in front of me. Slowly I put my finger on the trigger, just like we'd practiced at the indoor range the week before. Then everything froze and I felt like I was looking at all these targets in slow motion. From the corner of my eye I could see the other shooters watching me. I have to admit that the whole thing unnerved me a bit.

Later, after the match was finished, several shooters welcomed me to their club. They had been watching me on the first stage and relayed their conversation where one club member said to the other: "Is that gal EVER going to pull that trigger?" The other shooter responded with: "She's a brand new shooter. She'll pull the trigger sometime and she seems to understand gun safety." I eventually did pull the trigger. (I want to emphasize that with every shooting sport we have tried, the highest priority is ALWAYS on SAFETY!) I ran out of ammunition before I got to the last target, but I still felt victorious! I thought my first match went great considering that I had very limited experience shooting a gun. Yes, I was dead last in the match but I still finished the event. I started making new friends at the gun club and will always remember that my husband was very proud of me. I understood from my very first match that this was the one sport where coming out and being safe was all it really took to be a winner.

Moving On...

We shot IDPA for about a year, and then we started shooting another type of pistol match called International Practical Shooting Confederation (IPSC). This pistol shooting sport includes more physical movement such as running while engaging targets. Shooting the slower IDPA matches gave me the confidence to try IPSC. We'd been shooting IPSC about a year when we saw our first 3-gun match, which incorporates a pistol, shotgun and rifle. For those of you who don't know the difference between the shotgun and rifle, both are referred to as long guns. I've put some information on the differences between each firearm in the chapter titled "Lingo For Ladies." Every shooting sport we have tried encourages novice shooters to go slowly until they are confident about what they're doing. At our first 3-gun match, I shot it just like I did my first IDPA match. I ended up in last place but I didn't care. All the other competitors, along with the range officers, were very patient and helpful.

Over the last few years we've gotten addicted to the different elements and challenges of the 3-gun game. Now we take our vacations based on the matches where I can shoot my .40 caliber semi-automatic pistol, along with my 12-gauge shotgun and my AR15 semi-automatic rifle. Each gun has been a combination of a birthday, holiday, or anniversary gift. Over the years I've accumulated some nice guns and gear. It all fits me, not my husband, and that's important to a woman! I feel that each woman needs to have equipment that fits her properly. In case you were wondering how all the cleaning and repairs are done to this equipment, I have to admit that I don't do any of it. My husband (a CPA by trade) enjoys the technical "stuff," including loading our ammunition and cleaning our firearms. Some of my friends like Lisa Munson and Kay Clark-Miculek genuinely enjoy the technical aspects of how guns run. I have to admit that when a gun conversation gets technical to me, it sounds like: "blah, blah, blah." Several of the ladies I shoot with do clean their own equipment. While I respect their abilities I still don't want to learn about cleaning or repairing guns. I just want to shoot guns and have fun.

Princess Power...

If I didn't mention it before then I should tell you that basically I'm a princess, complete with a tiara. The men from my home range, Pima Pistol Club in Tucson, like to tease me about being a "crew supported" shooter. Besides my husband, I have to thank Salim Dominguez and Bill O'Hanlon. They are very patient with this particular princess and they rarely ever whine when I'm constantly asking them for help. I think you'll get a good laugh looking at the picture of the princess golf-cart decked out in hot pink trimmings. The driver with the bag over his head is Bill. He was a good sport about driving me around in the pink cart for five days at the United

Deb with driver, Bill.

States Practical Shooting Association (USPSA) national pistol championships. I usually have on a variety of pink shooting shirts since this is a good color for me. That was supposedly confirmed by a color analysis I had done a number of years ago. As a recent Christmas gift my pistol and other parts of my holster were repainted in hot pink. In this golf cart picture I'm not wearing pink. Instead I'm wearing another of my favorite shirts from the Second Amendment Sisters Foundation that says: "Firearms, The Ultimate In Feminine Protection." Their web site is in the Resource area.

While Bill is my patient driver, it ends up being Salim's duty to help my husband keep my guns running. Building friendships with other shooters is a good thing for more than just gun care. In a recent conversation with several ladies who shoot in 3-gun matches, we decided that having someone else besides your husband or boyfriend as an instructor is a good idea in most cases. Thank goodness that Salim and Bill are both retired. This way they have some extra time to be the instructor and crew for this particular princess!

In all the different shooting sports the people I have met over the years are supportive of new shooters, especially lady and junior shooters. I have shot firearms at dozens of gun ranges throughout the United States. I find people in shooting sports to be friendly and considerate. For single ladies who are worried about maintaining their equipment there is usually a willing assistant at almost every gun club that I have visited. You need to join, get to know people and ask for help. Rarely have I encountered men who weren't willing to assist a new shooter with technical problems. You don't have to become a princess but just in case this appeals to you there are inexpensive tiaras available at most discount stores.

Through my princess title I've gotten other labels as well. A few years ago we were shooting at the Superstition Mystery Mountain 3-gun match (SMM3G) in Phoenix. At one stage I was required to shoot at a metal target about 60 yards down range. Unfortunately there was a small tree limb hanging near the target (I swear it was near the target!). I managed to trim that limb away with a few wayward shots. To this day I'm known as "Princess Tree Trimmer" at that match. My side of the story is that I was only trying to make the target easier to see for those on my squad who were shooting after me.

So if becoming known as "Princess Tree Trimmer," or by wearing a tiara which I do on occasion, I can show other ladies that shooting is fun then I'm fine with the whole prin-

Princess Crew – Front row – left to right – Salim Dominguez, Gary Ferns, Bill O'Hanlon – back row Princess Deb.

cess title. I'm not a princess in any of the other things I'm involved with like a wonderful group called National Association of Women Business Owners (NAWBO). Through my involvement in this club, and through other community organizations that I support, I often have ladies approach me about their desire to learn more about guns. Most of them are concerned that they don't have the technical background, or they might not feel welcome at a range. My advice to these women is to grab a friend and get involved in some type of gun education program. Several programs are discussed in the interviews; such as the NRA "Women On Target" events or the Annie Oakley program. After completing a gun education program start taking a look at what types of shooting sports your particular gun club may offer. If you're interested in a gun education program for your kids there are a variety offered through the NRA, the 4-H clubs, and also through the Boy Scouts. Web sites for these junior programs are listed in the Resource area.

CHAPTER THREE

Ladies Camp...

Every story has to start somewhere, right? A few years ago I was competing in a large pistol match at the Rio Salado Club in Mesa, Arizona. This is a great facility and offers a wide variety of shooting sports, including our regional IPSC pistol match. While I didn't shoot that well I did see several top national shooters and they seemed very nice. I noticed Lisa Munson, then a seven-time ladies national pistol champion, talking with some other gals. I was a bit reluctant to go up to introduce myself, though where this uncustomary fit of shyness came from I'm not sure.

Thankfully my shy fit passed fast so that Salim and Bill could introduce me to Lisa, who they knew from previous competitions. As they say, the rest is history because I was introduced to Lisa and she turned out to be an awesome mentor for me. She wrangled me an invitation to attend a ladies shooting camp that was held at the home range of shooting "icons" Jerry Miculek & Kay Clark Miculek. My article on the camp, originally printed in the USPSA *Front Sight Magazine* (July 2004), is on the next page.

The Original "Ladies Camp" Article...

The title of this chapter pretty much says it all as twenty-two ladies, from every walk of life and every area of the United States, gathered for five days in April 2004 to enjoy non-stop shooting at the Clark-Miculek range in Shreveport, Louisiana. It was a true family affair as the Miculek's turned over their bunk house (now referred to as the Hen House) along with other family homes in the area, to accommodate almost two dozen shooters, ranging from A to D Class. *(Let me insert here that to make competitions fair, IPSC, like many other clubs, provides divisions and levels for every type of shooter from Grand Master to D class and you compete at your own level).* From all of us campers, a big THANK YOU to Kay Clark-Miculek, our camp director. Hearty thanks also go to her daughter, Lena, who was our camp back rub expert. And I can't forget Kay's husband, Jerry Miculek, who cooked for us gals and did a gun cleaning and maintenance seminar. He even cleaned the pistol each evening for the camp princess.

Ladies Camp was Kay's idea brought up at the 2003 USPSA Nationals. Kay mentioned she wanted to generate a strong women's team, in preparation for the world championships, which are held every three years. By the time Kay left the USPSA Pistol Nationals there were already 15 ladies signed up who wanted to improve their shooting skills. I put Kay on the spot during camp and wondered if she would be willing to do this program again in the future. I have to give her credit that she didn't even flinch when she replied: "I definitely would like to do another event like this next year. There's not a lot of places or camps where the environment caters to competition shooters instead of tactical self-defense. I can see now that there is definitely desire on the ladies part to participate in another camp."

Kay Clark-Miculek received roses as a small gift
for being a great hostess for Ladies Camp 2004.
For more information on future Ladies Camp go
to www.bang-inc.com.

Besides Kay there were three other volunteer instructors
(Lisa Munson, Athena Lee and Julie Goloski). All of the
instructors were the picture of patience plus persistence,
and I enjoyed Lisa's remarks when asked why she decided
to volunteer: "I want to prevent other women from making
the same mistakes that I did when I started to shoot. I feel
that women need more specialized training as they seem to
have different types of problems than men do with target
acquisitions, reloading techniques and aggressive movement
to the targets." This feeling was reiterated when Julie added:
"The women instructors who volunteered here this week

did it because we want to help you learn how to help each other. There are a lot of good women shooters in the U.S. but there could be a lot more! By doing this camp I feel like I'm helping to get it going in that direction, so that these women shooters will go back to their local clubs and encourage new women shooters."

As camp went on I have to admit that Lisa and Julie had valid points. It became second nature to watch each shooter, note her mistakes, watch the instructors address the problems and then try to incorporate the skills for myself. One of our campers, Linda Ashton, mentioned: "I've been in a slump as a low C shooter, problems that I couldn't address and my husband couldn't address, but here at camp the criticism has always been constructive, not destructive, and I feel that with work I can become a B shooter." Like Linda I felt that I've been "stuck" as a low C shooter but the final day of camp we had the chance to try out some of our new skills at the "ladies only" match that was sponsored by Smith & Wesson right at the same range.

Smith & Wesson brought in several guns to be used at different stages of the match and their donations to the prize table were much appreciated by the 32 ladies who competed that day. I have to admit that I was a bit timid about trying out new guns but it turned out to be a lot of fun. After all is there anything better then shooting a lot of ammunition purchased by someone else? Not only did I shoot my first revolver at this match but I also noticed when running the other stages with my own gun that my draw time, target acquisition and my splits (*time spent between each shot*) were noticeably improved (gee, maybe practice does help?).

I also want to pass on to all lady shooters some advice from my camp roommate, Deb Keehart (B Class Limited

Ladies Camp 2004
...So many great gals and so much fun!

shooter and international competitor): "Shooting with other women strengthens my mental game. Being at camp this week reinforces my abilities and inspires me to go home and work harder. The support you get from other women is a mental boost and 90% of this game is mental." I agree with Deb that the mental aspect of handling a gun is probably the biggest reason we don't get more ladies out to shoot. I am going to make a concerted effort to personally encourage more ladies to come out and enjoy this great sport. After all, the quality of the gals you meet in this sport is outstanding!

I shared this view with another of the campers, Carol Klesser (D class), who started shooting in December 2003. I wondered about her experience at camp and Carol replied: "Shooting with other women is a big bonus to a new lady shooter. I haven't seen any power trips, no egos in the way, just women celebrating each other's successes instead of failures. As a new shooter I've enjoyed the nurturing aspect of this camp. It's been very team-oriented." Not only did we do the nurturing thing, but on the second day of camp I woke up wondering why my ribs hurt so badly. Turns out that my new Cajun Camper Cousins (Annette Aysen, Barbara Thibodaux, Wanda Miculek) had gotten me laughing so hard that I damaged myself!

I'd be remiss not to send along a big "YOU ROCK" to Lisa Munson. I was the last shooter let into the camp because Lisa offered to forgo her plane fare if Kay would take me into the program. How do you repay someone who gave you the opportunity of a lifetime? The way I'm trying to repay Lisa is that for the first time in five years of shooting I'm going to the USPSA Pistol Nationals and will try to do her proud! Most of my new gal pals will all be there competing. I'm confident they'll cheer for me, I'll cheer for them, and with any luck Kay Clark-Miculek will see that Ladies Camp was one of the best ideas she ever had!

* * * * * * *

For more information on camps available through Kay and Jerry check out the Resource area. I hope you enjoy the interviews that follow, as they were collected from lady shooters spread across the United States. Each of them shared information about their particular shooting sport and how they became involved with guns. To me these ladies are truly BABES WITH BULLETS!

CHAPTER FOUR

What Goes Around...

In the magazine article I talked about the camaraderie that ladies enjoy through the shooting sports. Starting out with what I call a "combo interview," this takes friendship in the shooting sports a whole step further. It's about two ladies and one of them is Lisa Munson, who I indroduced earlier. Lisa hails out of Marysville, Washington, and to say that she is a nurturing spirit is an understatement. Over the years I've noticed that she is very willing to share the spotlight on any of her achievements. Every time a reporter approaches Lisa at a big match she tries to get the media to cover shooters other than herself. I've heard her say again and again: "I don't like to read about myself; that's not why I shoot and that's not who I am." So in some ways this basically shy gal is coming out of her shell although she still maintains a very humble perspective about her fame and glory.

A competitive mini-dynamo (5'1" and please don't forget that extra one inch!) Lisa has been married for 24 years to her husband, Eric, and they have two children. While Lisa did not grow up in a traditional family setting it's easy to tell that her family and friends are the most important things in her life. She likes to recount the story that the first date she and Eric went on was an NRA rifle match, way back in junior high school. Lisa didn't start shooting the IPSC game competitively until she was in her late 20's. If you can tell

Lisa Munson, seven time national ladies pistol champion and a wonderful mentor to novice shooters.

I'm a big fan of Lisa's then you'd be right. I'm sure there are other sports where ladies help other ladies, but share with me another sport where national champions volunteer to train other beginners for little or no money?

When talking with Lisa I wondered who was one of her inspirations and she promptly replied: "Kim Gorham." It would seem back in the late 1990's Lisa was in a bit of a slump and considering leaving the shooting sports. About that time Lisa was contacted by the USPSA office. They were wondering if she would consider training a woman who had recently called their offices looking for assistance. The lady, Kim Gorham, lived in Bellingham, Washington, not far from Lisa, and so the connection was made. Kim wanted to learn more about the IPSC shooting sports and Lisa was willing to mentor her. When Lisa met with Kim she noticed that her new pupil, already in her late 50's by this time, was struggling with severe arthritis. Kim was game to try anything to the best of her ability and Lisa found a whole new reason to stay active in shooting sports. As Lisa shared with me: "How can you not be inspired when you watch a gal like Kim? She has physical limitations but the heart of a lion to compete and never complains."

Comes Around...

Kim, originally from Texas, never participated in any matches when she was married back in the early 1960's, though now she is divorced. She did more casual shooting with small-bore rifles and pistols. Kim continued to look for shooting sports to enjoy, participating in tactical and steel pistol matches. She had never done anything like IPSC but "better late then never" was Kim's motto. In 1993 at 53 years of age she decided to try this physically challenging shooting sport.

Kim started out shooting a 9 mm pistol and then acquired a .38 super "open" gun. To give you a simple description an open gun is compensated to have minimal or no recoil. There is an optical sight on the front of the gun, which helps you quickly acquire targets. Kim went on to win big matches in her C division in the American Handgunner tournament in 1996 and again in 2000. She then began competing at the Bianchi Cup match. This is considered a very challenging accuracy tournament and Kim calls this event "the classiest shooting match I have ever attended." Although she had competed in many matches from 1993 to 2002, Kim shared with me that Lisa was with her for her first big match in 1996. They were together again for Kim's last big match in 2002.

Kim also has high praise for Dan Jones. He was the range master at Custer Sportsmen's Club in Washington and her coach for the Bianchi Cup Tournament. (It would take another book to write about the different elements in the Bianchi match but I have listed the web site in the Resource area). Something that struck me with Kim's story is that the motto "what goes around, comes around" actually came true. Lisa

Notice the saying on this gentleman's shirt? "I Was Beaten By Kim." That would be Kim Gorham, an inspiration to other competitive shooters as she attends matches using her power scooter.

and Dan coached Kim. Now Kim instructs dozens of people each year in gun safety. She gives them free shooting lessons, lets them use her guns and provides the ammunition. I know Kim has retired as a pharmacist and that her arthritic condition makes teaching and participating in shooting sports difficult. Still she never gives up and enjoys staying involved with shooting sports, though now on a local level. I enjoyed doing this interview. It reinforced my belief in the generosity of people in the shooting sports, whether they are national champions or someone with a disability. It also proves once again that there is a shooting sport available for every person!

Something You Can't Find on the Internet...

I know there is a popular belief that everything we need we can find on the Internet. However, I still like making friends the old-fashioned way. I like to meet people, face to face, shake their hands and get to know them. That's how Beth Wingfield and I got to be friends. We met in April 2004 at the Ladies Camp and spent five days together in the camp bunkhouse (lovingly referred to as the Hen House). When I met Beth she was shooting a semi-automatic pistol and competing in IPSC competitions. Beth continues to shoot IPSC but has also gone back to shooting revolver through the International Handgun Metallic Silhouette Association (IHMSA), which is where she started.

To give you a little background, Beth did not have any experience with guns growing up. "When I was growing up girls didn't shoot guns, but times have changed," she shared with me. I couldn't agree with Beth more. Times have changed and the shooting sports across the nation need to recruit more girls, women, boys and men. The kinds of people who come out to shoot come from all walks of life. Beth is a good example. She has a bachelor's degree in music, although she currently makes her living as a corporate quality control technician.

In 1993 when Beth was 38 years old, she and Mike were settling into a new home near Atlanta, Georgia. Mike decided to join the local gun club and Beth remembers they had an argument over the $300.00 fee. She decided to go out to the range with Mike. Basically she wanted to see how their hard earned money had been spent. Once she got to the range, Beth had the opportunity to shoot a revolver. She went to a gun safety course and started shooting different matches, like IDPA, IPSC and IHMSA. Beth remembers: "Whenever I didn't have the right type of equipment to try a match someone was always very generous about sharing a gun."

Mike was thrilled that Beth got interested in shooting sports and felt: "The best way to get your wife to stop complaining about the money or time spent on guns is to get her hooked too." Beth looks back at the years before she started shooting and remarked: "If it weren't for shooting I'd still be going to work, coming home, taking care of our dogs and cats, cooking dinner, cleaning the house, then starting over the same thing the next day. Now with my shooting sports, and my friends at the range, I have so much more to look forward to."

Beth Wingfield: "When I was growing up girls didn't shoot guns but times have changed."

When Beth was still new to shooting sports she met Cindy Noyes. Cindy turned out to be a good mentor for Beth. They continued shooting together at the South River Range, outside of Atlanta, for four years. It was in 1997 that Mike was diagnosed with inoperable brain tumors. He received huge doses of chemotherapy and then the hospital sent him home. As Beth remembers: "Mike's brain was gone, it was fried, and it was like having a 200 pound baby to look after. I didn't know how I was going to take care of Mike at home, plus keep working and paying bills. I just kept praying." I think Beth's prayers were answered but in an unusual way. It would seem that Beth and Mike had made some great friends through their different shooting clubs. A group of these folks, including Cindy, came to spend nights with Mike while Beth worked. This went on for months and little by little Mike started getting better. Here it is seven years later and Beth has just finished getting Mike back into revolver shooting. Beth exclaimed: "I'm excited we're going to be able to shoot together again, I feel like I've been blessed in life." Too often we don't appreciate the blessings we get in life. To be living in the United States with our unique "right to bear arms" is part of that blessing!

CHAPTER FIVE

Where To Start?

I shared earlier that my very first match was at a local IDPA event. On occasion I still shoot that type of match but I think Melissa Kreutz may be addicted to this particular shooting sport! When she started to shoot back in 2000 she lived in New Jersey. Melissa grew up with a dad who was an avid hunter but she had never shot a gun herself. I relate to this story; it was the same scenario in my family. I hope more men, and women, will start taking their children to the range to introduce them to guns in a safe and fun manner. It would be a great activity for you to share together and it beats watching television!

When Melissa was in her mid-thirties her husband passed away. That same year she was visiting her dad in Utah. He took her to a local gun range and gave her a brief gun safety class. She shot about 50 rounds from a 9mm semi-automatic pistol. Melissa admits that she wasn't a very good shot in the beginning. Still, she enjoyed having a new experience that she shared with her dad. Shortly after Melissa was back in New Jersey she saw an "anti-gun" show on television. She got so upset about the misrepresentation about gun owners that she fired off a letter to the network defending gun rights. Melissa's letter ended up being posted on the IDPA national web site. She received several positive responses from IDPA members. She also received some marriage proposals, which she thought was pretty funny.

A Good Place to Start...

On her next visit to Utah, Melissa was watching her dad participate in a local IDPA match. After about an hour she remembered thinking: "I can do this (IDPA). Next time I'm coming with my own gun and gear." Back in New Jersey, Melissa continued to monitor the IDPA web site. Since no matches were available in New Jersey she decided to attend a match in Austin, Texas. Through the Internet Melissa became acquainted with Beverly and Marc McCord, active members in the Austin club. She couldn't afford the airfare, plus the match fees and a hotel bill, so the McCord's invited Melissa to stay at their home. When she arrived, the McCord's discovered that Melissa didn't have the right type of belt and holster for the match. Beverly, a talented holster maker, created a bright blue leather set just for Melissa.

Even after five years I'm continually amazed by the generosity that I see throughout the shooting sports. I enjoy seeing experienced shooters willing to take newcomers under their wing. Not only did the McCord's provide a holster for Melissa but Marc spent time teaching her gun handling skills. Then two other gentlemen stepped into the picture and made Melissa's week in Texas even more memorable. Ray Chapman, a former IPSC World Champion, and Thell Reed, a well-known Hollywood "gun specialist," spent time with her. They extended Melissa's gun education in ways that years later she still describes in grateful and glowing terms.

From her first match in Austin, held in 2001, Melissa never looked back. While she couldn't find a club in New Jersey she found a receptive club in Pennsylvania. It was about a

Melissa Kruetz shooting IDPA.

two-hour drive from her home and though it was early winter that didn't stop Melissa. She continued to drive to matches every month. Currently she lives outside of Philadelphia and works as a computer analyst for a fiber optics company. Even from her new home the IDPA matches are still a 90-minute drive away; that's what I call devotion to the sport!

Now Melissa has a boyfriend who shoots IDPA with her. Melissa summed up her shooting experiences when she said: "I've never been to a range where the men weren't encouraging, warm and friendly." In addition to IDPA Melissa and her boyfriend also shoot Bullseye matches at a local indoor range. The type of Bullseye matches that she participates in uses a lighter .22 caliber pistol. Bullseye competition is also in larger calibers and is a pure accuracy sport. Melissa feels that Bullseye shooting forces her to concentrate and discipline herself to make a good shot. With the .22 caliber pistol she doesn't worry about noise or recoil. As she said: "Shooting a .22 caliber pistol is not scary. You don't worry about shooting fast. You just take your time to hit the center of the target with every shot."

Melissa did suggest that if you want to get good at Bullseye matches that having a steady strong arm is critical. (So much for drinking several cups of strong coffee before I go out to shoot this precision match.) In addition to shooting at IDPA and Bullseye events Melissa also volunteers as a range officer for large matches in her area. One such match is hosted annually by the Glock Shooting Sports Foundation (GSSF). Every year it gets bigger and in August 2004 this event drew over 300 participants. Whether you are at a local match or at a big GSSF match Melissa has a suggestion. "Partner new women shooters with experienced women shooters. It helps alleviate the intimidation and anxiety so that it's a good experience for a novice shooter." I think Melissa's advice is excellent. Personally, as an experienced shooter I feel that by helping novice shooters I'm giving someone else skills for life.

Instant Gratification....

One of the gals from my local club, Melinda Cantor, recently helped me out. I decided to do a short video by way of introducing *Babes With Bullets...Women Having Fun With Guns* at different trade shows. Melinda agreed to be interviewed on film and she started talking about her favorite event. "Steel matches are my favorite because there's instant gratification when you hit the targets and they fall down." I agree with Melinda on the whole concept of instant gratification. I think that's the reason so many matches include some kind of steel targets.

Melinda arrived in Tucson from upstate New York about five years ago. I keep saying that ladies involved in shoot-

Melinda Cantor as she enjoys a local 3-gun event.

ing sports come in all ages, shapes and sizes. Melinda is only 5' tall and nothing seems to slow her down, not even a bad accident that permanently damaged her right foot and ankle. She may never set any speed records as she participates in a match but she is a very accurate shot. As my husband remarked about Melinda a long time ago: "There's not an ounce of quit in that gal."

When Melinda arrived at our local indoor range, a few years ago, she started competing in IDPA matches. She was very comfortable with her .45 caliber semi-automatic pistol. Next thing I knew Melinda was starting to shoot at the outdoor IPSC matches, and then she started with steel events. Now whenever we have a local 3-gun event, there she is! So I guess you could say that Melinda got "bit big by the shooting sports bug." In case you were wondering her interest in shooting sports came after her accident, when she was already in her thirties.

I know that Melinda has introduced ladies from her dental office to our gun range. She gives them a gun education class and shows them the different types of firearms that she owns. She adds: "I'm conscientious about not scaring the gals. I encourage them to try handling a weapon that is appropriate for their size and upper body strength." I think Melinda has the right attitude about introducing potential new lady shooters in a careful manner for their first trip to the range. I cover more details about going to the gun range for a successful outing in the chapter titled "Gals, Guns and Glory."

I also want Melinda to know that I admire her tenacity to participate in shooting sports. Even with her limited mobility she maintains: "You shouldn't let anything hold you back. Shooting sports are for everyone regardless of age and physical capabilities." Melinda recently married another member of our club, Matt Evans. I think it's great that they are enjoying shooting sports together.

So Many Guns to Shoot, So Little Time...

Melinda is only a sample of ladies who enjoy shooting sports that include steel targets. There are a wide variety of steel matches held throughout the country. Some of these matches are done at the local clubs with 10 to 20 shooters. Other steel matches are huge with hundreds of competitors shooting over four days. One of the largest steel matches is the World Speed Shooting Championships, sponsored by the Steel Challenge Shooting Association. This monster match is held out in Piru, California, each summer. It offers a wide variety of categories to shoot in like Open Class, Limited, Revolver, IDPA Custom, IDPA Stock, IDPA Enhanced, Iron Sight and Revolver. Then within each gun category there are still more classes like

Ladies, Pre-Juniors, Juniors, Seniors and Super Seniors. Even if you're a brand new shooter, there's always a class or division for you where you can start out at a comfortable pace.

Speaking of comfortable pace, for the first three years that I participated in shooting sports I did not take my competitions very seriously. I never let my husband video tape me while competing at a match. Why did I want to depress myself watching the video? I already knew I wasn't a fast shooter and sometimes I missed targets. Then I took a weekend gun training class where the instructor was adamant that participants had to see themselves on video. He used it as an aid to show us several things relating to drawing the gun from the holster. We also reviewed our footwork, as we would run from one shooting box to another. Things like reloading the gun while moving and target transitions were covered. While watching the video I was forced to admit that I balance like a flamingo on one foot when shooting at targets. I developed a bad habit of barely keeping the other foot on the ground when I leaned forward. Don't misunderstand me, I'm a safe shooter, but this off balance position does not make a person shoot faster, nor does it make you more accurate.

Since that class I decided that having a videotape to review isn't all that bad. I still wish they made a camera that made me look thinner, but that's a different subject. I regularly watch my match performances on video and make notes about things I need to practice. The next time I'm at the range, I look at my notes and try to make corrections. I don't let myself get crazy at competitions and for the most part I maintain a sense of humor about the whole thing. At big matches there is always an area, referred to as the "wailing wall," where results are posted with each competitors score. As you can imagine some shooters never leave this area but I've found that to be a waste of time. By the time the scores come out you've already done your best. If you didn't do your best this time then you'll try to do your best at the next match. When the ladies I interview talk about competing against themselves maybe now it will make a bit more sense on how we view our performances.

By the way, in case you are thinking that somehow I've become a national champion, you can let go of that thought. The IPSC scale of shooting starts at D and goes up to Grand Master. I shoot at a C level and I'd like to become a B shooter before my AARP card arrives. My good friend and mentor, Lisa Munson, is putting in a lot of extra effort to get me there.

CHAPTER SIX

Women Having Fun, Three Guns At A Time!

Before you start thinking that these gals are trying to shoot three guns at the exact same time let me reassure you that this isn't how it happens! Remember: SAFETY FIRST, and while there are three guns (pistol, rifle and shotgun) used through the match, you only shoot one at a time. In August 2004 my husband and I were taking our summer vacation by participating in the annual Rocky Mountain Tactical 3-Gun event. I love to shoot 3-gun events and my favorite location to shoot this type of match is the NRA Whittington Center in Raton, New Mexico. The Whittington Center owns and operates a 36,000 acre private facility that also has guest units to rent. Picture walking out of your comfortable lodging in the morning and off you go to shoot at the match, which is about four miles away from your housing. In this case a group of about eight of us plan this event together. We've gotten to be friends over the last five years of shooting 3-gun events together so the camaraderie in the evenings is wonderful.

Speaking of camaraderie, we come back to our big cabin to relax after a day spent at the range. If you think that fishing stories get wild you should hear shooters talk about how the "big one" got away! In other words the story is about

Princess Deb offers fellow 3-gun participant, Kelly Neal, dessert.

how a certain stage in the match was set to challenge your skills and a good running time with good scores just managed to get away. My stories at the match were more on the level of how this princess, acclimated to Tucson's 2,500 ft. elevation, struggled to run and shoot targets at Raton's 7,000 ft. elevation. There are a number of jokes, all in good humor, about my needing an oxygen tank when I got done running the long rifle stage. I also take a lot of sociable ribbing about how at the end of a stage I insisted the Range Officer haul me back up the big hill on his ATV.

I've shared with you that I'm a princess. But I should reclaim some honor as I make note that for the big matches I take care of all the housing arrangements. I have also mastered crock-pot meals, which is quite a feat for me as I'm not a very good cook. Each evening when we got back from the range there was a full dinner waiting for us. I manage a nice roast, potatoes and a vegetable, all cooked to perfection while we've been out having fun. I also try my hand at some kind of easy dessert. I'll share a hint on my baking; with enough whipped cream burnt edges are forgiven. Actually I should say most of the group forgives the burnt edges. My friend, Kelly Neal (better known in our group as Mr. Gourmet Chef) brings along a fire extinguisher just to aggravate me. In my opinion Kelly is one of the best 3-gun competitors in the nation. I let him aggravate me about my baking as long as he continues to help me on the range.

Grandmothers Shoot Too...

Besides the match at the NRA Whittington Center we also attend some other great 3-gun matches like the SSM3G, held in Phoenix each spring and the USPSA Multi-gun held early each summer. Between these different matches I've met some wonderful women. Most of them started shooting 3-gun matches as they reached their middle ages, just like me. One of the first friends I made was Sandy Phipps, who lives near Casper, Wyoming. We stay in touch throughout the year via email. She and her husband (Rocky) have been married for 25 years. They have four daughters and at current count two grandchildren. When I asked Sandy about her job title she replied: "homemaker, rancher and enthusiastic gardener." It would seem that along the way to 3-gun matches Rocky is good-natured about stopping their truck. He lets Sandy out to wander through gardening locations. I know from experience that if I requested my husband to stop so I could shop that his expressions range from pain to frustration. A gal can only take so much deep sighing, so obviously Sandy has done something right in getting Rocky's cooperation!

Sandy never participated in shooting sports until about five years ago when she was turning 38. Like so many women that I know, Sandy was too busy taking care of a family to be able to spend much time on doing something fun for herself. Now add in the amount of time it takes to run a working cattle ranch and you can appreciate why she didn't start shooting until a bit later in life. As their girls were getting old enough to be self-sufficient Rocky purchased Sandy a 9mm semi-automatic pistol. "I was scared to shoot the pistol. When it went off I jumped. Then the more I shot the gun the more comfortable I got with the whole thing."

Sandy started going to 3-gun matches to watch Rocky participate and started thinking to herself: "I can do this, I should have signed up and shot this match." So her venture into 3-gun matches started with virtually no experience with shotgun or rifle and limited experience with her new pistol. When they first started going to matches Sandy admitted that it was very hard for her since she is very shy. The Phipps live in a fairly isolated area on their 5,000-acre spread. Going into a city, which to Sandy means anything more then a couple of thousand people, makes her nervous. Some of her shyness has worn off now that she meets new shooters. As Sandy said: "Shooting has been great for my self-confidence. Plus it's quality time to do something together with my husband, just like we did before we had the kids."

Speaking from someone who has watched Sandy shoot her rifle I don't think confidence is a problem! She may only have a few years under her belt but it's obvious that she is "at one" with her rifles. Now she shoots an AR15, plus a .308 rifle, which is a big caliber. Sandy claims: "There are all sorts of ways to make rifles comfortable to shoot. The AR15 is a great rifle for a lady, easy to shoot, no recoil but the bigger .308 can also be set up to shoot the same way." With her bigger rifle in tow Sandy got a chance to participate in a sniper school program hosted by the National Guard

Sandy Phipps...a shy gal building
confidence through shooting sports.

a few years ago. She was the only lady out of 18 shooters
and on the last stage of the program they setup a 1,000-yard
shot. Sandy was the only person to hit the target 3 out of 4
times. Needless to say the other shooters were very impressed and it's just one more example of how well ladies
are suited to long range rifle. Sandy's advice to other potential lady shooters is: "You're never too old to try
something new, getting involved in shooting sports could
bring something positive into your life."

From Sandy's description of a busy ranch life I know the
number of shooting matches for her and Rocky are limited.
They also have to travel long distances to reach any type of
gun club. She described for me the range they setup right
off the back of their home and each week they host their
own shooting contest. Remember the Phipps have 5,000
acres so they are not endangering neighbors. They are con-

scientious about where their bullets go. Sandy impressed upon me that she and Rocky use all the same gun safety rules at their own home range that they would encounter at a regular match. I mention this since so many new shooters think that safety elements might relax after you've been shooting for a while and that just isn't true. As our novice shooters become more experienced we usually encourage them to continue on for more safety training. Continued safety training is something that Sandy and Rocky do as well, even out on 5,000 acres.

"3-Gun Calamity"...

Sandy isn't the only grandmother who is good with guns. I met Cheryl and Rod Current from Albuquerque, New Mexico, about four years ago. One of the first things I noticed is that Cheryl's hair always looks great, not just good, but great! If you sense a bit of envy then you'd be right. My hair usually looks like it's been styled by an eggbeater after I've been on the range for about ten minutes. Cheryl and Rod have two children and six grandkids. I recently met one of their grandson's, Brandon, and he has started coming with them to the different matches. I think shooting sports is a wonderful way to find some common ground between these two very different generations.

Common ground is what Cheryl was looking for when she started going to watch Rod participate in IPSC pistol matches in 1985. As she said: "I didn't like guns, I didn't grow up with guns, and I wasn't comfortable with guns. But I got tired of just sitting and watching Rod shoot. Taping targets gets old when you're not the one shooting at them." Cheryl decided she wanted to be part of the action and started shooting IPSC pistol matches with Rod in 1988 when she was 40 years old. Then in 1990 she became interested in Masters shooting, which uses three types of pistols. Getting these new pistols caused Rod some serious heartburn, although he claims he has no regrets. Masters shooting resembles Bullseye for its precision with a small caliber pistol at close targets. There is a slightly larger caliber pistol used for long-range silhouette up to 200 yards away. There is also Bianchi steel plate racks added to the Masters element.

During the interview Cheryl shared that two gentlemen, Floyd Wine and Bob Jackson, taught her how to shoot long-range pistol. She felt her experiences with long-range pistols helped with transition to shooting rifles successfully. In 1993 Cheryl gave Rod another surprise. She wanted to get involved in 3-gun tactical matches so she'd need a new pistol, shotgun and a rifle. Cheryl felt tactical matches were a big learning curve but she was up to the challenge. In 1995 she went to the renowned Soldier of Fortune national match (SOF is now defunct). This particular match was very physically demanding and as Cheryl said: "I got hooked on 3-gun because of SOF. It was never boring and when I stood at the starting area holding my AR-15, I was in heaven. I felt just like GI Jane." When I asked Cheryl which gun is her favorite she made me laugh when she responded with: "anything that goes bang." Rod admits that keeping up with all Cheryl's guns, in terms of keeping them clean and running, is a challenge. He thinks he's created a monster but claims he wouldn't have it any other way.

Cheryl and I share some of the same sentiments. We both enjoy shooting the guns but not having to maintain them. I realize that some gals will want to take me to task for being a princess but like I said to Cheryl: "I work 50 to 60 hours per week; in addition to that I take care of the house, the laundry, the yard work, the animals and the cars. If I have to work another 5 hours a week cleaning guns and loading ammo then it's just another job for me instead of fun." So for the guys reading *Babes With Bullets*, keep in mind that you want shooting sports to be fun for everybody. If you want a woman to join you at the range I don't suggest making it more work for her. Cheryl agreed with me and added: "From the beginning, when Rod wanted me to get involved in shooting, he promised that it wouldn't add another work layer to my already hectic schedule."

Cheryl has won some notable titles in 3-gun competitions, like the Ladies Limited Division in the 2004 USPSA Multi-Gun national match. She also enjoys shooting at the big annual Sniper Paradise Match. The rifle targets are 1,000 yards away and Cheryl claims: "It's so cool, there is so much satisfaction in hitting targets that are so far away." She enjoys being one the few women who shoot with approximately 80 guys. Rod laughs when he describes the reaction from the other male participants when this New Mexico housewife can out-shoot them. According to Rod, some of the men congratulate Cheryl when she places ahead of them. Other men walk away, shaking their heads about being "beat" by a housewife. When the Current's aren't on their way to another gun match, then Cheryl works as a dance instructor. She teaches ballet, jazz and tap. Cheryl has several young teenage dancers who have requested that she teach them to shoot. She and Rod are willing to bring the guns, ammunition and provide the safety courses as long as the girls bring one of their parents with them.

In case you're wondering whether Cheryl is an Olympic athlete type gal then you couldn't be more off the mark. I think she is an attractive gal but as Rod said to me: "Cheryl is like Calamity Jane; every time she goes to a match something weird happens." It would seem at one match some years ago Cheryl had to start out seated in a chair. Then when the timer went off she had to jump up to retrieve her gun and start shooting at targets. Rod started to laugh when he shared: "Unfortunately the chair stuck to her like glue and she was running down the course shooting at targets with this chair hanging off her rear end." Cheryl laughs about her different mishaps and admits that things like this happen to her all the time. Keeping in mind that Cheryl's road to victory has not always been a smooth one she says: "It's a sport, it's fun, even when things don't go perfectly the key is persistence, don't give up."

Not a Princess...

If you're thinking that we're all princesses then let me introduce you to another 3-gun addict by the name of Cindy Noyes. Cindy is anything but a princess and a true "worker bee." Words like gracious, quiet, and competent seem to fit her personality. Cindy is a computer programmer for a bank, married, has two children, and took up shooting sports in her 30's. Now in her late 40's Cindy is considered "the mom of Georgia IPSC." From the South River Gun Club, near Atlanta, she runs four monthly matches and a large section area match each year for hundreds of shooters. Cindy also organizes a large annual match with over 400 participants for the Glock Shooting Sports Foundation (GSSF). Like this overachiever doesn't have enough on her plate, she also shoots at IPSC and 3-gun matches. When asked which is her favorite, Cindy starts to glow. "I love 3-gun matches, I think I shoot shotgun the best."

Something else Cindy said during our interview caught my attention. "Shooting is fun and once a week we do a social event at our club." It turns out that Cindy's club has

Cindy Noyes...so many guns to shoot
and so many matches to put on!

a long-standing Tuesday evening potluck dinner. It is at these social events that old members and new members are made to feel welcome. I am a big believer that if you want more women and juniors to be involved in shooting sports then you need to make it more social. This doesn't mean it has to be a dance, so you non-dancers don't need to go into cardiac arrest. Something as simple as a pot-luck dinner helps put everyone a bit more at ease with a new environment. I cover more of this subject of taking ladies to the range for the first time in the chapter called "Gals, Guns and Glory."

CHAPTER SEVEN

Reach Out
And Touch...

We're not talking about touch someone, rather touching targets that are 1,000 yards away with a well-placed rifle shot. Nancy Crowley uses her bolt-action rifle in a variety of positions, taking targets that are 10 football fields away. This type of shooting sport is done along the lines of sniper shooting. Since I've seen Nancy compete at 3-gun matches I wondered why she was diverting off into the sniper shooting. Bottom line is that she loves rifle shooting of any kind. Nancy uses her AR15 rifle for the closer 3-gun targets, of 100 yards to 400 yards. Then for the matches with targets that are further away she goes to the larger .308-caliber bolt-action rifle. Nancy claims the .308 is more accurate with less moving parts then the lighter semi-automatic AR15. The AR15 feeds rounds continually, while the bolt action rifle is one bullet at a time so she carefully plans out each shot.

Scared of Guns...

I thought that maybe Nancy had been brought up with rifles but exactly the opposite is true. When we spoke she set me straight as she said: "I was brought up to fear guns and I never even touched a gun until I was 44 years old." Nancy lives on a small rural ranch outside of Albuquerque, New

Mexico, and as a side job raises hay for her animals. During the day she works as a corporate computer programmer. Before getting active in shooting sports Nancy competed in high-level dressage horse shows. As she was finishing her doctoral program (PHD) in computer science she didn't have the time to devote to her riding programs. Nancy admits she never thought about taking up any kind of shooting. She changed her mind late one night when working outside at her ranch. As a divorced gal Nancy felt: "I was too exposed being outside late at night. I didn't feel like I could take care of myself."

Nancy mentioned to a friend that she would like to learn something about self-defense. She remembers going out to the range with her friend for the first time and how badly her hands were shaking. I wondered if she was afraid that the gun would be too loud or too big for her hands? Nancy replied: "I was worried about the whole experience. I knew I had something deadly in my hands and I was scared that I would do something wrong." She started with a safety course and by the end of the first session Nancy was confident that she wanted to continue her education in firearms. Her next introduction to guns was when the same friend took her to a nearby gun show. They were going to look at a variety of guns to see which one would fit her hand the best. This was Nancy's first time to a gun show: "I had always been told that gun shows would be filled with people who were freaks. I was terrified to be at a gun show and was glued to Rod's side, but after wandering through the place I have to admit that everyone was polite and no freaks in sight."

Nancy bought a .45-caliber semi-automatic pistol as her first gun. She joined the Zia Gun Club, which operates the gun range outside of Albuquerque. Nancy started out in action handgun matches, which is like a slower type of IPSC pro-

Nancy Crowley, PHD...no longer afraid of guns that's for sure!

gram. She remembers her first match with humor since she missed most of the targets and ran out of ammunition on every stage. Even though she didn't do well she remarked: "The other shooters were all so nice and encouraging, I had so much fun and knew I had found a new sport to enjoy." Now five years later she "owns a lot more guns and I don't run out of ammo (ammunition) anymore." In addition to the informal action handgun matches, Nancy started competing in IPSC. Now she competes in bolt-action rifle, IPSC and the tactical 3-gun matches that were covered earlier.

Even though Nancy has a busy match schedule, she still makes time for self-defense programs. She continued with her NRA training and became a certified instructor. Nancy, along with other local instructors, now teach a weekend NRA course called First Steps Pistol and Personal Protection In The Home. These courses are done on a volunteer basis and over 80% of the attendees in her classes are women. Nancy is aware that most of her students have never shot before and claims: "The transformation from women who are scared in the beginning, into women who are confidently handling firearms by the end of class is very rewarding for me." In fact Nancy was laughing when she told me: "By the end of day two we (the NRA instructors) bring out a variety of firearms with ammo for the ladies to try. Then we can't get them to stop shooting! They want to try everything." The other point Nancy made about the courses she teaches is: "It's one of the few things I can do that makes a difference in someone's life. That's a good feeling for me." Now that Nancy has been shooting for a number of years she says: "I'm not afraid to tell people that I shoot. I value my life and my ability to take care of myself. While I respect people who choose not to defend themselves, that is their choice, not my choice."

As we were finishing up our interview Nancy shared with me a situation she encountered at work. One of the men from her department stopped her in the hallway and said: "I hear you shoot guns, and I just wanted you to know you don't look like a shooter." Nancy's reply back to him before walking away was: "What do you think shooters look like?" I'd like to answer her question with one of my own. I think people in shooting sports look like Nancy, they look like me, maybe they look like my husband or my brother. Or maybe people in shooting sports will look like you?

It's a Garand, Not a Grand...

I always thought my dad was calling this gun a grand, but it turns out the M1 rifle is known as the J.C. Garand. While most people may not be familiar with this rifle it had a rich history of military action during World War II and Korea. I know my dad, a Marine during World War II, was a history buff and enjoyed talking about the M1. It was about ten years ago that my dad and husband went to a Civilian Marksmanship Program (CMP) held at the Tucson Rifle Club. Through attending this class they received refurbished M1 rifles at a substantial savings. They were both excited about receiving their guns, which is something that Dean Lucy could relate to since he did the same thing. Dean and his wife, Colleen, both shoot their J.C. Garand rifles at various Midwest matches.

I was looking for a lady to interview who was active with the CMP so I put a request in through their web site. A few days later I got an email back from Dean Lucy from the Bristol Gun Club, located outside of Milwaukee, Wisconsin. Dean went on to share with me: "Colleen has shot in every J.C. Garand Match at Camp Perry since it started in 1998." He also added: "I think some of her (Colleen's) best times are while passing out all the food she brings for our club. This is truly a family and friends shooting event, like something from 50 years ago." I give Dean credit when his email ended with: "Colleen isn't the best shot but she did beat me this year for the first time and I'm her husband."

Considering that the M1 weighs almost 10 pounds, compared to my AR15 at a mere 6 pounds, I was intrigued by the idea that a gal would want to shoot this heavy rifle. I dialed the Lucy's phone number and got a chance to know Colleen. Then when I got her picture I have to admit she wasn't what I was expecting. At 5'11", 135 pounds, along with blonde hair and red fingernails I wondered even more why she picked a big rifle to shoot? Colleen admitted: "I don't clean guns, I don't load the ammunition, I like being feminine. I don't like to hunt but I do like to shoot together as a family." Family has always been a big thing in Colleen's life and as she grew up in Florida she explained that her childhood included camping, water skiing and all sorts of

Colleen Lucy shooting her M1 – J.C. Garand rifle.
This particular gun was introduced in World War II.

outdoor activities. She added: "My dad had guns and I grew up respecting them. I think today that kids don't respect guns. Their parents seem afraid or unwilling to educate them about guns. I think this is a mistake because children are always curious about things they don't understand."

Colleen met Dean after she moved to Illinois. They got married and started a family. I guess you could say that for the Lucy's, shooting sports are a family affair. They obviously practice what they preach about educating kids on gun safety. Colleen was proud to share that their son took 1st place last year in the Junior Division at Camp Perry while participating in the '03 Springfield Bolt Action Rifle match. It wasn't until Colleen was in her early 30's, when their son was old enough to go to the range that she started to shoot the M1. I wondered why she'd want to start with this more challenging type of firearm. Colleen gave me an interesting answer. "I got into the sport because I wanted to be the person he (Dean) came home excited to be with. He was interested in the M1, so I got interested in the M1 because it was important to me that we share something extra. I love being a mom and a housewife. I like looking after my guys; it doesn't work for all women but it works for me. I just wanted to be a little bit more."

Colleen gives credit to Dean for buying her the right equipment, like a good shooting jacket with a stiff back. She says that makes shooting the M1 a little less harsh for her. As you might expect Colleen has had several men request her help in getting their wives, or girlfriends, to come out to the gun range. She is more than willing to be the enthusiastic recruiter for new lady rifle shooters but gives everyone the same advice. "Start the ladies out with an AR15, which is a very gentle gun and easy for her to use. The worst thing you can do is start her out with a rifle that is too heavy or has too much recoil for her." I agree with Colleen and I've included that tip, along with many more, in the chapter titled "Gals, Guns & Glory." I've been saying all along that having instructors other then your husband might be a good idea. In Colleen's case she credits Dean, along with other club members, in being very good teachers. About the men she meets at other matches she said: "All the guys want to help and it's always constructive and encouraging, never negative."

We went on to talk about her experiences at the big matches held in Camp Perry in Port Clinton, Ohio. Seems that the Civilian Marksmanship Program was tied in from the original DCM program (Department of Civilian Marksmanship). This program was started and funded by an act of Congress back in the 1890's, as a way to encourage young men to shoot correctly. Then in 1996 Congress took away the funding and the CMP program, along with Camp Perry matches, were faced with difficult times. The NRA was holding several large national matches each year at Camp Perry. In terms of the M1 match there were only about 300 shooters participating. The Lucy's wanted to see this match continue since they felt the people involved in their rifle shooting sports are family oriented people. As Colleen remarked: "We didn't want to lose this great environment and all these great friends." In 1999 the matches at Camp Perry underwent reorganization; they started promoting several more divisions. Colleen also noted that more women and juniors started to participate as well. She was pleased to announce that at the match in 2004 there were over 1,500 shooters. The only disappointment was that even with an event of this size it still did not receive any significant media coverage.

I wasn't surprised about the lack of media participation at the Camp Perry "mega match." I think every big match needs to do a better job of cultivating reporters from all media sources. I suggest that each gun club have a PR director on its board. This PR person should stay in touch with a small group of local reporters, calling them on a regular basis, whenever there is something new or different at the club. My experience is that eventually you'll get some positive media exposure. The other thing that Colleen brought up that I want to touch on is how the Camp Perry match was revitalized, growing from 300 shooters to 1,500 shooters. It grew and prospered because of Colleen and other shooters just like her.

CHAPTER EIGHT

Cowgirl Up...

That's the phrase we use around our horses when one of us gets thrown off and we have to get back up into the saddle. I am lucky enough to have some great gal pals who join in all sorts of riding adventures with me. While we bicker like sisters, I know we're kindred spirits. Our husbands nicknamed us the "Rowdy Rangers" and we have matching shirts that read "Rowdy Rangers...We Attract Danger." After getting to know cowgirl Robin Bloom I think you'll agree that we need to add her to our group of Rowdy Rangers!

Robin is an active member of the Single Action Shooters Society, better known as SASS. Each SASS member has a western nickname and Robin's chosen alias is Rocky Meadows (SASS #18501). SASS is also known by the informal title of Cowboy Action. It continues to be one of the largest and fastest growing shooting sports groups across the United States. Back in 1997 Rocky's father was active in SASS. At one particular match he attended there was the normal Cowboy Action event and also an event called Mounted Shooting. This particular event incorporates horsemanship with shooting. He knew Rocky had been "horse crazy" since she was a child. When he came to visit her in Sacramento, he shared the mounted shooting story with her. Rocky, at 34 years of age, was interested in any type of sport that would finally get her on the back of a horse. She and her dad picked out an Appaloosa gelding, Chief, and started the training process involved in SASS Mounted Shooting. Just so you're not confused, this isn't a gentle trail ride. Think of a 1,000-pound horse at a full run, rider on-board handling a set of reins and shooting out balloons with a revolver. The balloon targets are set up on a course inside a big riding arena. The rider that has the best time running the course, along with shooting out all the balloons, wins.

Before you begin wondering about the sanity part of this sport, I would like to reassure you that the mounted shooting program is big on safety. The ammunition (rounds) used in these single shot revolvers is made up of small walnut pieces with a little black powder, rather than a heavy lead bullets. When the gun is fired the black powder discharges the walnut pieces, and these pieces are what pop the balloons. Rocky acknowledges that trying to get all the equipment, and gear together wasn't easy but advises: "Go to a mounted shoot to watch. If your horse is ready to compete but you don't have the equipment someone will loan you guns and ammo. They (mounted shooters) just want you to come out and have fun."

One of the things that attracted Rocky to this sport is that it is family oriented. Being a single mom with two children, she was trying to find something she could share with her whole family. Rocky mentioned several times that SASS is very safety oriented and spends time with its new shooters. She said that women and junior shooters are made to feel very welcome. In terms of the right age to start competing, the shooter has to be able to read and write to pass certain safety tests. SASS also sponsors a large scholarship fund for their junior shooters. I think any type of shooting sports scholarship is a great idea. This is probably just one of the reasons that SASS continues to grow so rapidly among families across the United States.

Rocky became involved with the SASS scholarship program by offering her services as a hair stylist at a variety of SASS matches and events. She'd cut and style hair for $20.00 per person, with every dime of the money going into the scholarship fund. Last year, at the big SASS convention in Las Vegas, Rocky was recognized with the Golden Star Award. It was given to her by the SASS board of directors, known as the Wild Bunch, for "exceeding the normal expectations of the cowboy way." I think Rocky has exceeded normal expectations in other ways as well. In 1998 she won the ladies title in the SASS World Mounted Championships held in Los Angeles. Considering that she only started to ride and shoot in 1997, the transition from novice to World Champion in one year was amazing. I shoot 3-gun matches well. That's where I've been fortunate to win trophies, although I doubt I'll ever become a world champion in any of the shooting sports games.

I wondered if Rocky was thinking about leaving mounted shooting, maybe doing something else in the shooting sports? Without missing a beat she replied: "Mounted shooting is my favorite event, it's fast and furious. I love the adrenaline rush and that will stay my first choice." Rocky's web site is listed in Resource area along with the SASS site. You need to check out the pictures that relate to the old western costumes that the SASS ladies wear. They are outstanding! Rocky told me about a SASS survey, where they polled their huge population of lady shooters. The survey came back that 80% of the gals participated in SASS because it was social. The social part was brought up again

Rocky Meadows, SASS # 18501. She doesn't look like a rough tough mounted shooter but she is!

when Rocky was talking about "camp hopping." Much like a big tailgate party before a football game, these participants go from camp to camp to sample different "secret" recipes. So not only does a SASS event involve shooting, but cooking and costumes as well.

I'm going to try to make it out to the SASS World Championships with a new friend, Penny Moore-Cramer, a.k.a. Sister Sara. The match is called End Of Trail, and starting in 2005 it will be held at a new facility that SASS purchased in New Mexico.

Sister Sara ...

I'm finding out that if you are a SASS member it's more than likely you know people from all over the country. I met Sister Sara (Penny Moore-Cramer) up in Phoenix when she and I were attending the same pistol match. Even though we weren't at a SASS event Sister Sara agreed to put on her "shootin' duds" for me so we could get a few pictures of her old west outfit. In case you're confused, there are different costume divisions within SASS. Sister Sara has a nun's habit but she also has several others, including the saloon dress she wore for the photo titled Past...Present... Future. It was the different costume divisions that got Penny involved fifteen years ago when she was only 21 years old. Her brother originally introduced her to the shooting sports and he still competes with her. A few years ago Penny started to hope that a special man would come into her life and she was laughing when she told me: "I custom ordered Joe (her fiancée') by praying. I asked God to send me a man who loved shooting sports. I met Joe at the range and he is also a member of SASS."

After we got done laughing about God's delivery of Joe, we started talking about the more serious subject of why Penny wants to become Sister Sara. She told me: "During the day I'm Penny, a para-legal by trade, though currently I'm the legal secretary for our county prosecuting attorney. At night and on weekends I'm Sister Sara, SASS #1710." Sister Sara admits that she wasn't that interested in competitive shooting but she did love the idea of dressing up. Now at 36 years of age she has put to rest the old-fashioned thought that if a woman looks good then she probably doesn't shoot very well. Sister Sara regularly wins her class shooting at local and regional matches.

I asked Sister Sara what keeps her interested in shooting and she replied: "The camaraderie within SASS is wonderful but that's not the only reason I keep competing. For me shooting sports have become a stress reliever. I focus on the targets and all my other everyday problems just fade away." We were talking about the reasons why SASS has become so popular and there are several like the costumes and the social events. Penny had another insight that I think is important for women when she shared: "SASS is about the old west with morals and values from the 1800's. When I'm at a match I can leave

PAST...PRESENT...FUTURE. Left to right...Penny Moore-Cramer (a.k.a. Sister Sara), Deb Keehart and Lisa Munson. A historical revolver, a current semi-automatic 9mm and an "open gun" with a scope mounted on the top.

my car unlocked. I don't worry about my purse or any of my other equipment being stolen. In 15 years of competing I have never encountered anything but old-fashioned good manners. My most comfortable and fun moments in life come when I'm at the range." Considering what Penny does for a living I agree that being able to get away from our modern day problems must seem like a relief.

Even at work sometimes her shooting sports becomes a topic of conversation. On a regular basis, women walk up to her at the office wondering if she'd be willing to go to the gun range with them. In several cases these ladies have had a bad initial firearms training experience. A bad first impression is usually because an impatient boyfriend or husband did not handle a novice shooter correctly according to Penny. When they go out to the range with her the atmosphere is different. "These women do great at the range. They just need to go slowly as they learn firearms safety. They continue to build confidence in their ability to handle a gun as they are given positive reinforcement." Since her outgoing personality makes her a magnet for these women Penny has decided to finish her NRA firearms certification program. I wonder if she'll do instructions in her Sister Sara outfit, her saloon garb or maybe just in jeans and a t-shirt as Penny? I know that Susan Laws, another SASS member, will only recognize Penny as Sister Sara.

Aimless Annie...

SASS is estimated at over 40,000 members. So you can appreciate why so many ladies have great stories when talking about their involvement in this old west style shooting sport. I read an article in *Women & Guns* magazine and noticed that Susan Laws, a.k.a Aimless Annie, was the writer. I emailed her and she was great about sharing information on how her "fun with guns" began ten years ago. It seems that Sister Sara also knows Aimless Annie since they both participate in the SASS old style western shooting matches (but not on the back of a horse!). Susan started shooting when she was 48 years old. She was introduced to shooting sports through her husband as they were looking around for an activity they could do together. They went to see a Cowboy Action match and Susan remarked: "It looked like something I could do with him. The people we met when we went to observe our first club match were friendly, encouraging and obviously out to have fun."

Susan pointed out that Cowboy Action shooting combines marksmanship and historical reenactment, using equipment (a revolver, shotgun and rifle) indicative of the 1800's. Susan's "pride and joy" are her matched revolver set of .357 Colt Peacemakers. For the other parts of the competition she carries a reliable pump gun and a Marlin lever action carbine rifle. Susan grew up in Southern California with a father who kept a variety of guns in the house. So while she didn't have any fear of firearms, she just never had much opportunity to shoot them. Then she got married and transplanted to Texas, where she didn't start shooting until her daughters were already grown. Now in her late 50's Susan and her husband currently live in the Texas hill country with a dog and two pet longhorn steers. I enjoyed the image of Aimless Annie in this western setting. Now visualize this western property, complete with a private Cowboy Action range. It seems that the Law's have built their own range so they can practice and entertain friends they have made through SASS.

Susan claims that Cowboy Action shooting is a sport that women can excel in at any age and continue playing as long as they like. She is articulate about what she gets out of her involvement in shooting sports when she said: "I learned to handle firearms with confidence and competence. I have become much more aware of the importance of an armed citizenry for the purpose of personal protection. Through involvement in the shooting sports, I have become more politically aware of government decisions which affect my right to bear arms and now have a better understanding of what the Second Amendment is really about." In case I didn't mention it before, it was through Susan that I was led to Rocky. I find that lady shooters are always willing to support other lady shooters, which I think is grand!

Same Song, Different Verse...

I think of shooting sports as one song where everyone knows the lyrics, maybe to the tune of "row, row, row, your boat." Sylvia Jackalone knows the song but her verse is different. She participates in Cowboy Mounted Shooting Association

(CMSA), which is a different organization then SASS. Actually CMSA was the original mounted shooting organization and several of its members, like Sylvia's husband Bob, have also participated in SASS programs. Sylvia grew up in Illinois, exposed to guns since her father hunted, though she never had the inclination to participate in hunting events. She went on to add that she never had much interest to do any type of sports.

Bob was the one always involved in a variety of riding events and introduced Sylvia to horses. When they got engaged he asked her if she wanted a ring or a horse? Sylvia decided on a horse. When I asked her why a horse, she replied: "I couldn't ride the ring and I always wanted a horse." While Bob got involved in western Quarter Horse events Sylvia was happy to go trail riding and took care of their family. They have now been married for over 35 years, with two grown boys and one granddaughter. She and Bob have been in business together over three decades, operating a hair salon for the last six years in Tucson.

It wasn't until three years ago, when Sylvia was already 54, that she decided to try mounted shooting. She watched Bob compete at a CMSA matches and felt the mounted shooting was like watching a dance. Sylvia stated: "The movements with the horse and rider are so poetic; it's pretty and smooth. I think it feels like ballroom dancing when you do it right." In trying to learn more about this particular shooting sport Sylvia requested help from Sandy Moore, a local Tucson mounted shooter. As time went on Sylvia continued her lessons with Annie Bianco-Ellett. She credits Annie with teaching her a technique called "self-talk." As Sylvia goes into a lesson or a match she tells herself: "I can ride, I can shoot, I can be better at this sport." Sylvia en-

Sylvia Jackalone riding Texas T-Bone at a CMSA event.
I think they are a beautiful team!

joyed sharing with me that Annie regularly beats most of the men at CMSA events and holds several Mounted Shooting World Championship titles.

Like so many other shooting sports there is a level for everyone. In Sylvia's case she started out at a walk and trot, shooting the balloons at Level One. Now she is at Level Two and says she'd like to make Level Three. We discussed moving onto a senior division in our respective shooting sports, since we are both over 50. I've decided we're going to call it something other then senior division. What do you think about giving it a title like AB for Aging Beautifully instead? Recently I saw the picture of Sylvia competing on her horse in a CMSA event in a lovely black and white Spanish riding costume. I think that Aging Beautifully suits her much better than senior. Sylvia's enthusiasm for this event is contagious. I signed up the "Rowdy Rangers" for a mounted shooting lesson. Wish us luck!

CHAPTER NINE

PULL!

So far we've been sharing stories about pistol and 3-gun matches. However, one of the dominant shooting sports for ladies are the wide variety of clay programs that use a shotgun. I'm still a novice at this shooting sport which uses a clay disc, that resembles a small Frisbee, for a target. I've shot skeet and trap a dozen times, and sporting clays once. Even with my limited experience I can see why gals become addicted to these fast moving games. The command the shooter gives to launch these targets is PULL! It's exhilarating when you hit one and it disintegrates into several pieces!

One of the first times I handled a shotgun was when I signed up for a ladies trap league. I had an old 20 gauge semi-automatic shotgun, which was a good choice for this inexperienced shooter. In the beginning I kept thinking: "This shotgun is going to hurt me." Like a lot of gals I assumed shotguns would have more kick. As long as you tuck the shotgun snugly into your shoulder and keep it pressed against your face the recoil is minimal. Imagine my surprise when I shot a whole round of trap, which consists of 25 shots, and incurred not one bruise. (As princess I appreciate guns that don't bruise me.)

And speaking of the princess title I think I found something better – I found a DIVA! More to the point I found

Cheryl Waldrum, originally from Oklahoma, but transplanted to Dallas. Cheryl is a petite gal, a retired rock & roll singer, and a dynamo with a passion for shooting sporting clays. She's also very active in a great ladies shooting club called the DIVAS. The club motto is "boots and spurs are not required but a tiara is a must." I heard about Cheryl from another DIVA member, Kathy Sedlecky. Kathy talked with me and shared a few experiences from her 50 years of being involved in shooting sports. It was through Kathy that I was introduced to Cheryl Waldrum, the DIVAS, and several other people in the shooting sports industry. So to Kathy I send along a note of thanks and I look forward to meeting you in person along with the other DIVAS!

The DIVAS originally started in Dallas back in 1999. This club now has over 700 members in 47 states and 14 foreign countries. This club continues to grow with its founder, Judy Rhodes, at the helm. According to Judy the DIVAS love the smell of gunpowder. This is a good thing since these gals shoot in a variety of competitions, using pistols, shotguns and rifles. As Judy shared with me: "The DIVAS are all about attitude and quests. Believing in women for the future of the outdoors and shooting sports is a wonderful journey. We (the Divas) are all about women helping women, women teaching women and women supporting women." Judy's description of club activities encompasses charity events, an active social agenda, plus a long list of shooting matches and programs.

In fact catching up with Cheryl to do an interview was a challenge. She was on a fast track coordinating the DIVAS semi-annual fall clinic. The clinic held in the Fall 2004 introduced over 120 new lady shooters to pistols, rifles and shotguns. For this particular event Cheryl lined up four shotgun instructors, four pistol instructors and four rifle instructors. As Cheryl lamented: "We could have easily used twice as many pistol instructors."

You may relate to Cheryl, since she wasn't born into a shooting sports family. At 46 years of age Cheryl married Hugh and as she said: "The man had guns, every type of gun; it was a little spooky." Over time Cheryl came to understand that Hugh loved the technical aspects of guns… why they run…why they don't run…what it takes to make them run, the same way a golf fanatic loves his golf clubs. From the beginning he taught Cheryl to treat every gun as though it were loaded, which is the number one "golden" gun safety rule. Within a year of the marriage Cheryl started to think: "This is crazy, I'm living in a house with all these guns, and I should learn how to use them." She decided to start with pistol training and participated in IDPA matches for the next two years. Along the way Cheryl also became an NRA certified instructor.

Though Cheryl admits she was frightened in the beginning, she never gave up. She continued to learn about other types of shooting sports like Sportsmen Team Challenge. This sport uses three guns, like a .22 caliber pistol, a rifle and a sporting shotgun. Teams of three people each shoot a different gun in a relay, for a combined time and score. A very different type of shooting sport from the tactical 3-gun matches discussed before. Cheryl enjoyed this event but after she began shooting sporting clays she was "hooked." Sporting clays encompass a total of 50 up to 100 clay targets. The clays come in different sizes and different colors, though the one thing they all have in common is that they are moving fast! Cheryl's word to sum up her passion for sporting clays is "addicted."

Cheryl Waldrum...She shoots, she sings and she's a proud member of the DIVA'S.

During our interview Cheryl and I shared a few princess and DIVA stories. Just for the record she doesn't clean her guns either. "I paid good money for these nails and I'm not ruining them," she stated. Cheryl continues to enjoy shooting sporting clays at least three times a week and for her the practice is paying off. She won the 2004 Ladies National Sporting Clays title in E class. Unfortunately Hugh wasn't able to cheer her on at this big match since he passed away after a long illness in March 2003. Cheryl claims that it was the DIVAS who come through for her during Hugh's illness. They continue to provide Cheryl with moral support, a chance to continue competing, and the most important thing – camaraderie.

From Divas to Annie Oakley...

I like to think of the DIVAS as a group of modern day Annie Oakley's. Speaking of Annie Oakley, there's a program in Arizona that's named after this famous lady! My husband

and I decided in October 2004 to attend a large pistol match at the Ben Avery Range, located near Phoenix. I hadn't been to this particular range before and was impressed at how efficiently the Arizona Fish & Game department runs this beautiful facility. As we were driving through the range I kept seeing signs stating: "Annie Oakley Event, Every Thursday, 7:00 p.m. to 9:00 p.m."

The Annie Oakley program turned out to be the brainchild of Don Turner, long time "wizard" of Arizona Fish & Game. Back in 2001 he had tried to get another program going called Guns & Gals. Unfortunately this original program didn't seem to attract much attention. Not willing to give up on their gun safety mission Don and his team went about getting permission from the Annie Oakley heir to use this positive female trademark name.

From the moment they started the Annie Oakley program in early 2003 it was a huge hit. Approximately 4,000 ladies have gone through the training series in 18 months. In addition to the ladies program Don and his team simultaneously offers a juniors program. They have processed over 5,500 kids in the same 18 months. Now that's what I consider a successful program! After talking with Don and Bill Kelsey, also with Arizona Fish & Game, I want to share with you how their marketing ideas made the difference:

➤ The Annie Oakley program is exclusively a ladies program. Men are not allowed to stand around and watch the event. Men are encouraged to help with the junior program or take a different course themselves.

➤ Instructors for the Annie Oakley program are mostly women volunteers, all are NRA certified instructors and/or range officers.

➤ Each Annie Oakley participant gets complimentary hearing and eye protection. They get to keep these items after the program is completed.

➤ There is a 45-minute orientation where each lady gets a large notebook that contains information about gun safety issues, descriptions of different firearms, firearms cleaning procedures and miscellaneous range guidelines.

➤ After the orientation the ladies go out to the range. Here the instructors have lined up several types of weapons for the ladies to try. Each weapon is a .22 caliber so that the noise and recoil is minimized. The new shooters can try a semi-automatic pistol, a revolver, and several types of .22 caliber rifles.

➤ The participant gets a punch card that allows each of them to receive 500 rounds of ammunition on a complimentary basis. (I admit that I still get excited when I shoot someone else's ammunition for free!)

➤ The participants also get a free admission to the range to come back and try shooting on another day.

➤ The same type of program is offered to the juniors with a very nominal fee charged.

For that many people to attend the Annie Oakley program I was curious how it was marketed in the community. Let me introduce you to the Outreach mobile unit that is owned by Arizona Fish & Game. They take this unit to different schools throughout the Phoenix area and cover gun safety with kids of all ages. Inside the mobile unit they have an air gun range. Kids get a chance to understand how targets are scored and they put into practice the gun safety rules they've just learned. Each child receives a pass for a free day at the Ben Avery range and also receives an Annie Oakley brochure to take home to their mothers and sisters.

As a mom I know that kids are interested in the "forbidden items," like guns. The mission statement for this program is impressive and like you might think it's related to gun safety and education. Take a look at their web site, www.basfaz.com, also located back in the Resource area. As Don said during our interview: "The Annie Oakley program is not a social club. It's an upside down funnel. First you teach women about gun safety and then you introduce them to shooting sports. As they go along with the program the funnel of opportunities just gets bigger for them. The more they know about guns and gun safety the better it is on their children." Something else Don said struck a chord with me when I asked him what advice would he give other ranges: "Be interested in the long term goals of recruiting new shooters and don't just stop at putting on a one day seminar. Have other programs ready to share with anyone who attends a gun safety course." I think the Annie Oakley program is well thought out and obviously well received. Maybe other states will eventually emulate them. I also think Don Turner must be a very special kind of man. He has been with Arizona Fish & Game for 30 years and is still enthusiastic about introducing women to shooting programs. He'll be a hard act to follow when he retires.

Speaking of the Annie Oakley program I met an interesting gal who has participated in this event. Her name is Marsha Petrie Sue and according to her own description she was a "city girl through and through," having grown up in Los Angeles. Now Marsha is a retired corporate executive, living in Phoenix, with a resume that includes Westinghouse and other Fortune 500 names. I don't think the term retired fits her since Marsha is anything but retired; maybe I should have said reborn. These days Marsha makes her living as a trainer and motivational speaker, plus she is an accomplished author in her own right. I got her latest book, *Shopping For Mr. Right*, for my two single daughters to share. In case you are also looking for your own "Mr. Right" I've included Marsha's web site in the Resource area.

Marsha, now 59 years young, met her husband through an on-line dating service about a dozen years ago. She described their relationship with these words: "We agreed in the very beginning of our marriage to stay open to each other's passions. My husband's passion was guns and hunting." I wasn't sure exactly what Marsha meant so she gave me an example: "As my wedding gift he bought me a beautiful 20-gauge shotgun. I gave him tickets to the theatre and symphony." I started getting this mental picture with Marsha, attired in her designer clothes and emeralds, at the gun range. It turned out she was a woman of her word and as she said: "I wanted to honor my end of the bargain. I went out to the Annie Oakley program at the Ben Avery Range to learn about guns in a safe and constructive manner."

I wanted to include Marsha because the interviews are mostly devoted to women in organized shooting sports and she doesn't fit in that group. Marsha and her husband enjoy using their guns for the occasional round of skeet and target shooting, but mostly for hunting they do together. In Marsha's case she and her husband don't belong to any formal gun club, rather they are their own club of two. I know there are thousands of women shooting with partners in the same manner. My hope for you is that this shared interest in shooting sports, or in hunting, makes your relationship stronger.

CHAPTER TEN

Women On Target...

Carol Leonard is the gal I interviewed for the NRA "Women On Target" campaign. I think there are some similarities to the Annie Oakley program. It's all about women encouraging other women to come out to the range to have a good time. Carol was originally from Kansas, then ended up in New Mexico when her father was transferred there for a job in the 1970's. She remembers guns in her family since her dad was a hunter but she didn't have any "hands on" experience. The "hands on" part came when she moved back to New Mexico in 1985. In Carol's words: "I had two young kids to raise alone after the divorce in 1985. So I moved back to New Mexico to be near my family. I thought it was important that my children have a father figure in their lives, especially my son."

Eagle Scout...

In 1996 Carol's son was trying to achieve his Eagle Scout, the highest merit achievement available through the Boy Scout program. He decided that his Eagle Scout project would relate to introducing the Boy Scouts to gun safety, education and maintenance. The project would also include shooting competitions and improvements made to his local gun range. For his Eagle Scout program to be accepted by the Boy Scout organization there had to be an adult active in the scouting program that was an NRA certified instructor. Three guesses on who stepped up to the plate to be the NRA instructor? Besides spending time going for the NRA certification, Carol related to me: "I don't know who worked harder, my son or me, since it had to be an adult handling the concrete mixer, the chop saw, and the chain saw. I just know it was time well spent with him."

Carol continues to teach the upcoming Boy Scouts the same gun safety program that she taught for her own son. Then beginning in 2001 she started teaching the NRA program "Women On Target." The program utilizes men and women volunteers teaching gals gun safety, making them familiar with a variety of firearms and giving them a chance to shoot. Carol teaches this program every year and this past summer they had reached their maximum group capability of 45 ladies. They ended up having to turn away dozens of ladies due to range restrictions. Whatever they're doing with the Otero Practical Shooters Association (OPSA) at their home range in Alamogordo, New Mexico, it's working!

In Carol's opinion the statement "you're never to old to learn to shoot," is true. At her last "Women On Target" program she shared with me: "Our youngest lady shooter was 18 and our oldest lady shooter was 83. The oldest shooter was a riot and she was a good shot besides." In addition to becoming a certified NRA instructor Carol also received her certifications for Range Officer, Pistol & Home Protection and the Refuse To Be A Victim program.

Besides her involvement with the NRA Carol decided to start participating in SASS events. That's the same old west style shooting sport that was highlighted in the chapter titled "Cowgirl Up." Carol credits her mentor at the club, Robbie Roberts, with encouraging her to try this fun event. "I couldn't afford to buy my own equipment. I couldn't even afford the ammunition so the guys at my OPSA club loaned me their equipment and even loaded ammo for me," she said. These contributions from her club were only part of the picture as she explained: "Robbie started coaching me so I could compete in Cowboy Action. The members of this club are so supportive of lady shooters that at times it leaves me stunned. I've even been president of this club, now I'm the treasurer, and one year our entire gun club board had all female officers."

For some of you ladies who think you won't be welcome at a range, or at gun clubs, I suggest you revisit that thought process. Maybe that was the attitude during my mom's day or even back in the 1970's. Now when I talk to women, they feel that the men at their gun clubs go above and beyond the call of duty to make women and junior shooters feel welcome. For Carol, the loan of equipment and coaching were only part of the story since along the way she's had some other great moments. A few years ago a couple from her club, Ken & Becky Lane, presented her with a custom holster and a gun belt. Ken did the leatherwork, ingraining a motif of barbwire and roses. Since Carol's SASS alias is Alamo Rose she said: "This gift was a great fit for my personality." Now that her children are grown (her son is a Marine who recently got married and her daughter, along with two grandchildren live up in Seattle) Carol continues her volunteer work at the range. On occasion she gets to participate in Cowboy Action matches, resplendent in her Alamo Rose customized costume.

I wouldn't worry that Carol has too much free time now that her children are grown. Her other full time job is as a department manager for Wal-Mart. She gives her store high marks for letting her stay active in the community. Carol assists

NRA's Eddie Eagle teaches gun safety to elementary school kids. Carol Leonard teaches gun safety to women and high school students. What a great team they make!

with the NRA Eddie Eagle/Gun Safety program hosted at the Wal-Mart parking lot. She also does volunteer work for the store program called "Good Works," which donates money to various charities in her community. Through Carol's extensive volunteer efforts she was selected as one of a dozen women in her community to receive the prestigious award "Woman of Merit." The NRA also recognized Carol with a special plaque as the 1st Runner Up for its prestigious Sybil Ludington Award. This national award is given each year to the woman who exemplifies the NRA goals on gun education and Second Amendment Issues.

When the newspaper came to do a story for her different awards she posed for the picture attired in her Alamo Rose outfit. The title of the story was "Carol Leonard, On Target In the Community." She gets a big laugh that the reporter was struggling to keep up with all her community activities and admits: "The awards have been great but they aren't why I volunteer. I volunteer because I want to make a difference in my community." In my opinion, I think Carol makes a difference, a big difference!

Romance with Revolvers....

This title reads like one of my favorite historical romance novels. Maybe the theme would be cast back in the 1800's, when revolvers were the name of the game. We already know that women used them to protect their homes and families for centuries. Today women still love their revolvers. I have to admit that I have had very little exposure to revolvers. That changed in April 2004, I shot one of my first big revolvers with Jerry Miculek coaching me along. I couldn't have asked for a better coach since Jerry holds dozens of world championship titles, all won with a revolver. It was during this same time frame that I met Annette Aysen. I love to hear her talk with her Cajun accent and I enjoy watching her handle a revolver too! She moves along gracefully shooting, reloading, shooting some more, and then at the end of a stage she evaluates how she did. For the most part I'd catch her laughing and making remarks about how much fun she had as she was shooting.

Annette has been married for over 30 years and lives with her husband outside of New Orleans. She did very little shooting growing up, though she admits to being a "tomboy." Then in the late 70's Annette's husband, Elliott, became involved in different shooting competitions. Annette decided she didn't like being left at home so she purchased a six shot revolver. First she started shooting in tactical events and then in the early 1980's she shot at bowling pin matches.

For those of you questioning bowling pins being used as targets just picture those skinny white things set on racks at a distance. I've tried this particular shooting sport and have found that bowling pins can be a very crafty target to hit! According to Annette: "You really have to concentrate on the front sight of the gun and hold steady if you want to get the pins down in a fast time." Obviously holding steady is something Annette excelled at since she ended up as top woman at some big bowling pin matches. Unfortunately in the mid 1980's there was a bad recession in the oil industry and this directly affected Louisiana. The Aysen's, like so many families in their community, were affected by this recession. The extra money for things like shooting sports wasn't available any more. For the next 17 years they raised their son, continued to work hard, and waited for better times to come.

I can empathize with Annette's story. I was raised in Michigan, where the automotive industry seemed to have an endless cycle of good years and bad years. Every time the cycle started again my family was affected in one way or another. There just wasn't enough time, nor money, to devote to the shooting sports. Like the Aysen's we didn't start shooting until our kids were older and the demands on our time a bit less. Now that our girls are grown we plan most of our vacations around big shooting matches.

For the Aysen's, they started going to steel matches to shoot together again in 2001. Annette admits that things had changed so much in 17 years that at 45 years of age she wondered: "Can I still compete with my revolver? All my friends have changed over to shooting semi-automatics instead of revolvers. Should I change over to a semi-automatic pistol too?" Annette decided to stay with a revolver and refresh her skills since she felt comfortable with that particular firearm. She knows her gun and her other equipment are old-fashioned but they still work. So instead of investing her money on new equipment Annette decided she'd rather attend matches. With that thought in mind the Aysen's went to the American Handgunner event in 2003.

The American Handgunner is a large pistol match, held every summer for one week in Montrose, Colorado. Since Annette had rarely left Louisiana, this was a big experience for her. She shared with me: "Every walk of life was there from all over the world, shooting every type of handgun imaginable. That's what makes it so wonderful; the experience is exceptional." Though Annette didn't win at this event she felt she did well in 2003. Then in 2004 she placed even higher when they went back for the second time to American Handgunner. Annette passed on some other thoughts I think housewives will relate to when she said: "I started shooting to do something with my husband. I found out that I enjoy it and the matches (competition) give me something to look forward to. I like keeping my brain engaged and feel that the challenge of shooting sports is good for my over-all health. It's a mental and physical boost!"

In talking about the different shooting clubs Annette mentioned her membership in the following groups:

➤ National Rifle Association (NRA)
➤ International Confederate Organization of Revolvers (ICORE)
➤ United States Practical Shooting Association (USPSA)

These clubs, along with several others, are listed in the Resource area at the back of the book. Also listed in this area is a great web site, www.brianenos.com, containing a huge selection of shooting sports information, including material on USPSA. I bring up this particular web site since it has a very good on-line forum regarding shooting sports. I shared the thought with my husband about adding a similar forum to my web site but make it just for ladies. He started laughing so hard I thought he was going to hyperventilate! He reminded me that I get frustrated trying to operate the satellite system to make the television work. While I know web site design is not my strength, I don't think it was particularly kind on his part to tell me that I'm "technologically challenged." So maybe in the future I'll figure out a way to make a ladies forum happen at the www.babeswithbullet.net site after all.

Tutus, Toe Shoes, .50 Cal

I'm not talking about 50 calories; I'm talking about Wendy Henry and her passion for .50-caliber rifles. I originally thought this big rifle wouldn't fit a professional ballet dancer. In my mind it didn't blend with tutus and toe shoes, but I was wrong. Wendy says: "All the things that went into my being a professional ballet dance are the same things I use to shoot a .50-caliber rifle. From being physically fit, using self-discipline, having stamina, preparation for a recital or a match, those are all the things I use to shoot my rifle." Wendy left the professional dance world and has three kids ranging in age from 21 to 10. She's 45 now and estimated she started shooting a .50-caliber rifle about six years ago.

After living for several years outside of Philadelphia she moved with her children to the Pocono area of Pennsylvania following her divorce. Wendy was introduced to the sport back in 1998 through her current boyfriend, who had been shooting rifles for several years. He took her out to the NRA Whittington Center in New Mexico to watch him compete in the .50-caliber World Championships. They got there a few days before the match and John, her

Wendy Henry...Professional ballet dancer, mom and active member of the Fifty Caliber Shooters Association (FCSA). This picture was taken of her instructing a ladies program called *Women In Scope*, which was hosted by FCSA.

boyfriend, noticed her interest. He asked her if she wanted to try to shoot the gun and her immediate response was: "Yes, I want to give it a try." She ended up shooting dozens of practice rounds to get used to the rifle and entered the match a few days later. What's even more amazing is that she took a 4th place in her division at a national match. Not too shabby for a newcomer! Wendy admits she's hooked on rifle competitions, though she is also involved in hunting programs that utilize the skills she's developed with her rifle.

To bring more women into rifle shooting Wendy also runs matches for the Fifty Caliber Shooters Association (FCSA). She is very encouraging to other women thinking about trying her sport and said: "Women are very talented with rifles in general. You don't muscle the gun. You finesse the trigger, which seems to be something ladies are good at." In May 2004 she was a volunteer instructor for the "Women In Scope" program hosted by FCSA. Over 100 ladies attended this program and when the attendees first got there Wendy sensed most of them were afraid of guns. "Many of these ladies had never touched a rifle before and they had never been educated about them." Wendy said. Once they had the opportunity to learn about the different rifles they were enthusiastic about shooting them. Wendy shared with me that in her opinion: "Shooting guns is like driving a car. Cars and guns are safe to use, a great tool for having fun, if you are trained to use them correctly."

I have never thought of guns and cars from the standpoint of a similar educational process. Now that Wendy planted that seed in my mind it seems to be taking root. I know there must be some good bumper stickers we can come up with; as an example how do you like this one: "I'll swap you one of my guns, for one of your cars. Both must be comparable in value and running correctly at time of swap. Either one can be used as a weapon."

CHAPTER ELEVEN

Soap Box Issues...

The relationships and interviews discussed in the previous chapters are important to me. The issues we'll cover during "Soap Box" are also important, though a bit more on the serious side.

Another Way to Look at Things...

For years a vigorous debate has raged from strict gun controls to no gun controls, from protecting our Second Amendment Rights to rewriting the Constitution of the United States. One of the gals I interviewed sent me a bumper sticker that read: "Ignore Your Rights and Eventually They Will Go Away." Well, that pretty well sums up my greatest fear. I believe that if you aren't part of the solution then you're part of the problem. My Second Amendment Rights are important to me. My participation in shooting sports, and encouragement of other women or juniors to join me, is how I'm part of the solution.

Ask yourself some simple questions. Do you basically believe what you've seen on television, or read in your daily paper, in reference to gun control issues? Would you accept whatever the media tells you about cancer or the war in Iraq? No, you wouldn't. You'd want to know the facts first! Aren't your constitutional rights just as important? On several occasions I have had women walk up to say to me:

"I'm afraid of guns." They feel this is a fair evaluation and I don't think it is; I think it's an avoidance technique. I appreciate that they are frightened of guns, but I would rather educate them about firearms, rather than compromise any of my constitutional rights.

The NRA, and other organizations like the Second Amendment Foundation, have extensive web sites relating to the U.S. Constitution and the U.S. Bill of Rights. There are several books available on these issues as well. Try to find a book, or articles, that are historically factual and not written in a biased fashion.

P.C.

I'm starting to think that P.C., the overused tag line for Politically Correct, has become an escape route. Maybe P.C. really means Please Conform, or in other words don't say or do anything that other people may find disagreeable. Personally I'm okay with people agreeing to disagree. I'd be okay if P.C. meant Polite Conversation. My mom always told us kids that manners didn't cost anything, which was a good thing since we didn't have much money growing up. When I'm talking to people who might not agree with my pro-gun stance I understand it's important to maintain good manners.

I had been participating for quite a while in shooting sports before I became comfortable sharing with people that I was involved in any type of activities that involved guns. Over time I grew confident of my shooting skills and read a bit more about my Second Amendment Rights. I decided that not standing up for what I believed in was just wrong! Sandy Froman, incoming NRA president in 2005, summed it up when she said: "People think that voting is all they need to do to protect their rights and actually that's only the start. Americans need to do something to preserve their rights every day." When I shared with Sandy my philosophy on

P.C. (i.e. Please Conform) we agreed there might be more truth to that statement than we wanted to consider. With that in mind I haven't excluded interviews on hunting sports or domestic violence because I'm concerned with being politically correct. Rather there are several good books and magazines already relating to these issues for ladies. For instance if you have an interest in hunting programs for ladies then I would recommend the NRA magazine, *Woman's Outlook*. The other hunting source that I have listed in the Resource area is United Special Sportsmen Alliance (U.S.S.A). If I get the opportunity to write another book about amazing women involved in hunting programs I'll definitely include Brigid Donahue, founder of U.S.S.A

I also don't want to mislead anyone into thinking that I've done a complete study of every type of shooting sport. Just how many shooting sports I was still missing became obvious to me when I spoke with another gal, Sue King. Sue is the "grand dame of hunting" on the NRA board of directors and participates in several types of shooting sports. In fact her team won a national championship in Sportsmen's Challenge. When we were talking I mentioned that every time I thought I had a list of all the shooting sports I'd find a few more I never knew existed. Sue started to laugh and said: "The number of shooting disciplines is enormous. You'll have to write a second book!"

Debbie's Wish List...

I have wishes and concerns just like all of you. One of my concerns is that we need more women and juniors involved now to insure that shooting sports are around in the future. To get more involvement in shooting sports I think there are both political and cultural differences that need to be addressed. I have some thoughts I'd like to share with you:

➤ I don't consider myself an enemy to another American, even if their political views are different then mine.

➤ I believe in the Pledge of Allegiance

➤ I believe in the U.S. Constitution and the Bill of Rights.

➤ I've spent time in Europe, and while it's a nice place to visit, I don't want to live there.

➤ I do not believe that the United Nations is interested in what is good for Americans.

➤ I'm confident I'm capable of taking care of my family and myself if necessary.

➤ I wish more American women would find the courage and confidence to be educated about guns.

This last wish has a humorous twist. As a corporate meeting planner I meet and speak to hundreds of new people each year. On occasion my shooting sports will be a topic of discussion. Basically the response is the same each time as people say to me: "I hope if something bad happens in my (home, work, whatever) that you're standing next to me." The funny thing is that I wish they were proficient with a firearm and could take care of themselves.

The Lighter Issues...

As you may have guessed I'm a fan of the shooting sports in this country. Being a fan doesn't mean that I don't see room for improvement within each gun club, or at every gun range. You, the new shooter, can help make those improvements and your voice counts. I am hoping that the match directors you talk to, along with the ones I might be able to reach, will take this information to heart in the good spirit in which it was delivered.

Lena Miculek (left) and Julie Goloski (right). A junior girl enjoying time at the gun range with a several time national pistol champion.

. . . .

"Shooting sports offer a unique opportunity for women, especially to build confidence and set goals at every ability level. It is something women can pursue individually or as a family. Shooting sports offer a place where those who participate are embraced by a strong community dedicated to safety, sportsmanship and having fun."

– Julie Goloski

. . . .

Partial list of Julie's titles include...
- 2004 World Speed Shooting Ladies Limited Champion
- 2004 International Defensive Pistol Association Ladies National Champion
- 2004 United States Practical Shooting Association Production Ladies National Champion

➤ Keep in mind that you are the person that every supplier involved with the shooting sports wants as a customer! Suppliers include gun manufacturers, ammunition companies, holster vendors, clothing retailers and the list continues. My goal is to encourage more women to try shooting sports. You, along with junior shooters, represent the demographics that the firearms industry as a whole would like to see participating (and buying more) in the future.

➤ For every world or national champion shooter there are literally thousands of novice or average shooters quietly supporting the industry. I know some shooting sports insist that the champions be divided up onto different squads at big matches. I feel that this is an excellent idea. These champions are quite often sponsored by gun companies or gun related industries. The goodwill generated by the champions, along with a positive reflection upon their sponsors, by shooting on regular squads is an important issue. All of us in the shooting sports, including the champions, need to continue good public relations. It's a simple formula: good public relations = new shooters.

➤ It is the novice or average shooters, like you and me, who support matches through entry fees. We are a large part of who pays for the prize table winnings that participants take home. If you get a chance to shoot with a champion take advantage of it, don't be shy. Enjoy learning from the best in the world and read about range etiquette in the later chapter noted as "Manners Matter." It will give you hints on when is a good time to strike up a conversation with fellow shooters and when you might want to wait for a better opportunity.

Okay, much to your relief I'm getting down off my soapbox. I hope both the potential new shooter, and the person introducing you to guns, will read the next chapter. My goal is to share what I know and to continue learning along with you.

CHAPTER TWELVE

Gals, Guns
And Glory...

I've listed some useful tips on how to make taking a new shooter to the range into a successful event instead of a dreaded one. I don't claim that these hints are the "be all and end all" in gun safety or firearms training. Besides the programs mentioned, there are several training academies located throughout the United States. These academies, or training centers, do a good job teaching gun safety and gun handling techniques if you can afford a three, four or five day course. There are also a number of good books and videos that graphically show a step-by-step approach to shooting. The tips I offer are oriented toward encouraging women to come out and try shooting for the first time. Or in some cases you might be trying to get past their previous "less then wonderful" experience in gun handling and recreate a positive memory.

Setting the Stage...

I believe that timing is everything and so is preparation. Popping up at breakfast with the thought of "running out to the range for a while" isn't the way I'd recommend approaching this event. I can almost guarantee that this "hit and run" method is going to compromise an already busy day for her. I'd suggest giving the new shooter a specific date for an experience you'd like to share with her. So onward with thoughts to make your new adventure a great one!

➤ Make sure there are at least 3 hours allotted, and then include the extra travel time to/from the range.

➤ The time frame should allow you to do something social on the way back home. Maybe stopping for ice cream? Could you join up with some other members from your local gun club for a social chat over a meal? If the day at the range ends on a social note my experience has been that ladies remember that the event began well and it ended well. The day at the range turned out to be a wonderful new adventure that she got to share with other people.

➤ I don't suggest rushing home so she can fix dinner and catch up on laundry now that she's been at the range all day. All this does is reinforce her thought process that going out to do something with guns makes her life harder. I would rather see a positive memory that going to the range is fun!

➤ Take a leisurely drive out to the range and point out landmarks along the way. The new shooter can then feel comfortable that she could find the place on her own.

➤ If possible I'd recommend going to an outdoor range for the first exposure to any type of shooting sport. The noise at an indoor range can seem heightened and the shooting tables/bays can feel a bit tighter for a beginner. The exception to this rule is a new modern indoor range, like the one at Scottsdale Gun Club.

➤ If the only range available is indoors then I recommend calling ahead of time to see what type of hours they run. Explain that you are a new shooter, or you are introducing a new shooter, and you would like to come out during a slow time. See if the staff seems helpful or harried. (Gun store employees run a number of the indoor ranges, so there may be a limit on store personnel who could be on hand to help a new shooter.)

➤ Call the outdoor range for their hours. I'd get their web site address if they have one. Usually from the web site you can get a map (Yes, a map! It lowers the aggravation level for everyone in the car). Find out when different clubs are shooting their weekly or monthly matches. Maybe you'd like to make your first trip to the range when there is a match going on that interests you. This could be a good idea, especially if there are other ladies or juniors who participate in the match. Don't plan to stay for the whole match. The last thing you want to do is bore your new shooter.

➤ Don't bring babies, or other small children, to the range when you are introducing a new shooter. If you are taking a junior shooter I recommend making it a "one on one" event. If you're not the one shooting a gun or learning about guns then the range is a boring place. I've also discovered that childcare at a gun range is a difficult task, even for the most proficient mothers. Keep in mind that this is supposed to be fun, not a hair-raising event where everyone is trying to keep track of the kids.

➤ Don't bring your pets with you to the range. I can't tell you how many people think that going to the range will be a nice outing for Fido and it's just not true! Some dogs are very gun shy, quivering and quaking in the car throughout the event. This is not a reassuring sight for the new shooter and typically it will mean a fast end to your trip. Other dogs, especially hunting breeds, love going to the range. They want to wander everywhere, including going down range while the match is going on, which obviously is not a good idea. If you tie them up at your vehicle, the barking and whining can be profuse, which other shooters don't appreciate.

➤   Before going to the range on what you think is a "non-match" day I'd call one more time to ask if there are any other miscellaneous things going on. I've gotten out to the range with a new shooter only to find the local police were having a training day. It wasn't on the web site but things change all the time. Believe it or not a gun range can be a very busy place. Just because you don't go there on a regular basis doesn't mean that it doesn't get used.

➤   If you get to the outdoor range and it's packed with several people using different types of guns you may not even get your new shooter out of the car. For someone with no experience, or limited exposure to guns, the noise can be very loud and frightening. Keep in mind that this new shooter doesn't know any of the other people at the range. As yet there is no trust factor built up that these strangers will be careful with their guns. The trust factor comes later as they watch how the gun safety and gun range rules apply to everyone all the time!

➤   You've arranged a day to go to the range with your new shooter. If it's bitter cold, miserably hot, or raining, then do me a favor and don't go! My dad and

Amber Stubbs getting her first pistol lesson from
a patient, and competent instructor, Gary Ferns.

brother seemed to enjoy duck hunting in the pouring
cold rain. My experience is that most women don't
seem anxious to learn about guns if they are freezing,
wet, or sweating. I know this presents a problem if the
weather doesn't cooperate on the one day you have
plans to go. Maybe you could have a good indoor range
as a Plan B. If there isn't a good Plan B, it's better to
postpone the trip than make that first impression a last-
ing bad impression.

➤ You FINALLY make it to the range on a beautiful day
with your new shooter. Make sure you go to the range
office and sign in. Usually there's an on-site range
master, or attendant, who will give you instructions on
where to shoot. If you neglect to sign in then the range

attendant will usually come by, reminding you that you weren't following proper procedures. A new shooter is already wondering if they are in the right place. If they get a hint that maybe they aren't welcome then the chances of getting them back to the range again are not as good.

➤ It's rare to get a cranky range master but it does happen. Don Turner, from Arizona Fish & Game, wrote an article about this problem. I'll try to find it and post it on my web site. Keep in mind that the range master or attendant is <u>not</u> a representative of the shooting sport you may be considering.

➤ Find the right area of the range for the type of firearm you will be using. If there are a few shooters in the same area then move down. Give yourself as much space as possible. Before you get out of the car make sure the new shooter has comfortable eye protection and ear protection.

➤ I'll cover eye protection first since I see so many gals and juniors put on these big safety glasses that keep sliding off their nose. I found safety sunglasses (poly carbonate) at a discount store for $8.00, which is a bit more then regular safety glasses cost. These glasses were 100% UV protection and they fit my face since they were ladies glasses, not found in the construction/hardware department. I got the same type of glasses with a yellow tint and I frequently use them in low light situations, like an overcast day. As you get more serious about shooting sports, then definitely invest in some top of the line shooting glasses. A number of people I shoot with have prescription glasses made just for their shooting sports.

➤ I keep in mind that some ladies don't like to crush their hair with the heavy ear muffs/protectors. Try to find the ear sets that have a thinner wire band going across the top of the head. I wear junior ear protectors, which fit me better than the big muffs like the ones my husband wears. I wear double ear protection. This is a combination of the headset and small custom rubber earplugs made years ago at a gun show for about $35.00. The beginners I've worked with tell me they like the double ear protection to keep the noise at a minimum. I would also recommend electronic ear protectors, which are pricey but worth the money. I don't feel that the little ear foam pieces are adequate for long-term hearing protection.

➤ Before you even un-bag the first gun I advise that you tell a new shooter about terms like down-range, cold range, cease fire, etc.. More terms like these are covered under the heading noted as "Lingo for Ladies." Sometimes when you talk to a new shooter she doesn't always relate to things in the same fashion a man would. A few months ago I had a new lady shooter with me and I told her: "go back to the car and put on your ears." She walked over to the car, checked in the mirror, and let me know that she had both earrings on. I then explained that her hearing protection (her "ears"), were sitting on the front seat of the car. We got a good laugh out of the experience but it did remind me that we take certain terms for granted after being involved in the shooting sports for a while.

➤ With every new shooter we go through some of the common terms and then we start on the basic gun safety. I like to give a new shooter a laminated card to keep that lists the four "golden" rules of gun safety and these are:

First Rule – A gun, <u>every gun</u>, is always loaded. Every time you pick up a gun always treat it like it's a loaded gun even if you think it's not.

Second Rule – Never point the gun at something you are not prepared to destroy. Always keep the muzzle in a safe position.

Third Rule – Keep your finger OFF the trigger until your sights are on the target. If you are moving with the gun keep your finger OFF the trigger.

Fourth Rule – Always be sure of your target and what is behind it. Bullets can go through a lot of different materials, even wood. Aim at and fire at a safe backstop.

I have faith in these laminated cards. Last year I noticed that one of the older students had put a magnet on the back of the card and had hung it on the front of her refrigerator. There it was, the four rules of gun safety, hanging with the coloring book drawings from her granddaughter. As her granddaughter comes to visit the new drawings go onto the refrigerator. At the same time they go through the four rules of gun safety together.

➤ Eye and ear protection are in place. Gun safety rules have been covered. Retrieve your gun bags, along with the ammunition in the boxes or cans. Put it all on the range tables or counters provided. Place any of the gun bags facing down-range so when you eventually get the gun out it won't be pointing at your new shooter. Keep in mind that even though you know the gun is not loaded, a new shooter won't know that. Their new rule, the one that you just taught them, was that every gun is always loaded!

➤ Last year while at the range I saw a guy arrive in a nice sports car. He made a big deal out of telling me: "My girlfriend has finally come out to the range." As she got out of the car she had on the wrong type of clothes, wrong shoes, plus her eye and hearing protection were too big for her. The boyfriend started loading up her arms with different kinds of guns to carry over to their shooting area. She didn't look very comfortable carrying the guns and promptly dumped them on the closest shooting counter. Of course the boyfriend started to howl about possible damage to the scope on his rifle. I think it's better to let the new shooter sit down in one spot and let them watch as the equipment is placed on the table or counter. It also gives them an opportunity to look around at the range, maybe locate a bathroom. You can turn the new shooter into a pack animal later but not on the first time at the range.

➤ In terms of appropriate clothing and footwear for the range I usually tell the ladies that it's definitely a jeans and t-shirt event. I like to look nice but it's more important to be comfortable. Quite often the range will have wooden benches or metal chairs to sit on, which can snag silk or other nice materials. I don't suggest anything with a deep V or U neckline and I'd recommend long-sleeves. I'd save any special clothes, like a nice sundress or cute shorts outfit, to wear at gun club social events. I'm not trying to come across as an ultra conservative dresser. I just want to make sure that going to the range is a fun experience and dressing right is part of that experience.

➤ When the trigger goes off and the bullet is sent down-range there will be a small used casing, which is referred to as brass. This small piece of brass will on occasion bounce off the shooters chest or arms. Remember this piece of brass is supposed to be ejecting from the gun, so nothing is wrong. The brass is hot in the beginning and you do not want it traveling down the front of a shirt or hitting anyone on a bare arm or bare thigh. Even if the new shooter is standing next to you when you shoot, a piece of brass can still hit them. Make sure the new shooter is a safe distance away from brass coming out of the gun or that they are prepared for it when they are shooting. The less surprises the better when a new shooter is at the range for the first time.

➤ In terms of footwear I'd go for tennis shoes or hiking boots. There are all sorts of little metal objects or even small pebbles on the ground at a gun range. I've seen ladies arrive at the range in all sorts of footwear including high-heels and sandals. I'd also suggest dressing in layers so that as the day warms up layers can be taken off but still keep your arms and chest protected. Make sure that flying hair is caught back with clips, ribbons, a snug visor or hat. Having hair whip across your eyes is irritating, especially when a new shooter is trying to hold onto a gun with both hands.

➤ I'd start a new lady or junior shooter with a low recoil gun, like a .22 caliber handgun. I don't put ammunition/bullets into the gun right off the bat either. I like for the new shooter to see that the gun is empty. Sometimes I'll show her the empty gun three or four times. That way she becomes used to treating the gun like it's always loaded but I'm establishing a trust factor with her. Keep telling her that the gun won't go BANG until she's ready for it. I even go so far as to watch any other nearby shooters, especially those shooting loud rifles like my AR15. It doesn't bother me when I'm shooting it since the noise blast is going away from me. However shooters standing anywhere near me are not "happy campers." So pay attention that your new shooter isn't going to have an unpleasant experience when someone next to you shoots a loud gun.

➤ I agree with how my friend, Deb Keehart, introduces the gun to the ladies by shooting it in front of them first. That way they can see how Deb, all 100 pounds of her, handles the gun plus they get acclimated to the noise. I shoot a few slow rounds at the target and then I show the new shooter an empty gun. I even place the ammunition down the bench away from us a little ways. (Last year one of our new lady shooters worried the bullets would "magnetically jump into the gun" when she wasn't looking.) Fear does strange things to people and the only way to lessen fear is through education.

➤ Then pointing the gun down-range I like to setup her shooting position. We put her arms up and pushed out in front of her, so she is holding the unloaded gun up, not pointed down at her feet. Try not to make your arms poker stiff and keep your shoulders down. Most ladies don't like to stick out their butts; still to balance your weight a bit better you need to stick out your butt just a bit. Then bend your knees and lean forward. This way your weight is more forward than leaning back. If you watch a mom holding a baby on her hip the normal stance is swayed more back or to a side. In shooting a gun you want the stance to be more forward and centered equally over the two feet. Don't despair if it doesn't feel natural at the beginning; it comes with time.

Amber Stubbs (left) with Raya Ferns (right). Raya finally got her best girlfriend, Amber, to come to the range with her. They even posed for this picture so they could share this memory for years to come!

➤ This is a good time to also check and see if the new shooter is right or left eye dominant. There are simple steps for doing this in every handgun "101" book. Once the new shooter has a comfortable and balanced position let her pick up the unloaded gun. I let them get used to pointing it at a target. From behind the shooter I stand with my hand on their back, just so they know I haven't deserted them. Men don't seem to like or need that extra touch but most gals or junior shooters do. If you are wondering where I picked up most of these techniques it's from watching my husband over the last five years. He is very calm, and never acts like he's in a hurry. I've never seen him push a new shooter faster than their level of comfort and he always does successful introductions.

➤ Somewhere in this mix we explain what a front sight and rear sight look like on the gun. Keep in mind that quite often a new shooter won't even understand that there is a front sight. I setup a target close to the new shooter, maybe to start only 10 feet away. I encourage them to line up the sights and I let them dry fire (no bullets in the gun) a few times. They get the feel for the trigger pull and the "click" that it makes after it's finished. I even rack the gun for them as they do dry fire, always careful to take the gun from them in a safe manner and hand it back to them in a safe manner. A number of the ladies who come to the range don't have much hand strength. Making them grab the slide on the top of the gun and pull it backwards is hard for them. I should mention that's how it works on a on a semi-automatic pistol. Revolvers, also known as "wheel guns," are easier to use. The last thing I want is for any gal to think they aren't strong enough to handle a gun. There is a firearm out there for every ability level! I do everything I can to make handling a gun feel comfortable to the new shooter. Eventually after some dry fire practice I'll load a few bullets for the new shooter to give it a try. By this time they have usually relaxed enough to enjoy putting a hole through the target or knocking down steel.

➤ I didn't mention it before but make sure you take little breaks off and on during the first shooting experience. This isn't a race. It's supposed to be fun and educational. I'd also make sure you have something to drink like water or a power drink. I'd stay away from carbonated soft drinks, especially if it's hot outside.

Caffeine and sugar don't produce side effects that are necessarily helpful to a first time shooter. The other thing I always take along is a canvas folding chair, and possibly an umbrella if it's going to be a hot day. Some ranges don't have these extra amenities and your new shooter will be more comfortable if there's seating and shade available.

That brings me to why I'm a big believer in first bringing out a low caliber handgun. You can always bring out more guns later, including rifles and shotguns. Let your new shooter get a bit more comfortable with trying new things at an unhurried pace. I can't count the number of times I've seen people bring out a new lady shooter and place a big caliber pistol in her hand. Then I've seen this gun filled up with self-defense ammunition that has a ton of kick. Kick is what it feels like when the gun is fired and a shock wave travel up the shooters hand.

If the gun is significantly too big or too heavy for her hand she'll struggle holding on to it from the start. She'll probably end up holding it stiffly away from her body and won't have a good stance when she pulls the trigger. All these things spell "I don't want to shoot this thing any more. It's loud, it hurts my hands, I thought it was going to hit me in the face, I want to go home!" That's assuming of course she didn't drop the gun because it frightened her.

About two years ago I was at the range and I watched a guy hand his wife, obviously an inexperienced shooter, a big pistol with magnum loads. I asked him why he was doing that and he said: "This gun is what I keep in the house for self-defense so that's what she has to get used to." WRONG! She shot one bullet down range, dropped the gun and sat in the car trying not to cry. I told him the chances were slim that she'd ever use the gun for self-defense after that experience. The good part of this story is that my husband and I convinced the gal to get out of the car. She went with us to take a short course in gun safety and gun handling. She had a chance to shoot a lighter caliber gun with much better results. Moral of the story is that if a person wants to take you (a new shooter) to the range, make sure first that they are qualified to make this a fun and safe experience for you.

Let's assume that you've got a new shooter interested and she's even getting some good shots on the target. Maybe she seems willing to try another gun, maybe a 9 mm pistol or a .38 revolver. I never jump from a small caliber gun to a much bigger caliber gun without going step by step through the different options. It only takes one bad experience for her to look at you and say: "that's enough, I'm not having fun anymore." When I tell my husband I'm tired that's his clear signal that our practice session is finished. Don't ruin a good thing. When you see that your new shooter is getting tired finish this first session, even if you haven't done everything you've planned. Remember that the amount of adrenaline that it took for that new shooter to spend a few hours at the range probably wore her out.

This more pampered approach to firearms education might not work for military training or law enforcement. But my mission isn't about that type of training. It's about is getting more women to try shooting for the first time and to get them to come back! I hope that these few hints help make it a glorious day at the range for any gal.

This is one of my favorite quotes. It paints a great picture of how I'd like to arrive in Heaven if I'm given a choice. I tried to find the original author without success. I wanted to confirm that a busy woman wrote the quote.

"Life is not a journey to the grave with the intention of arriving safely in a pretty and well preserved body, but rather to skid in broadside, thoroughly used up, totally worn out, and loudly proclaiming... Wow! What a ride!"

– Author Unknown

CHAPTER THIRTEEN

Manners Matter...

This chapter relates to gun range etiquette and some hints on how to become a good competitor. It will help the new shooter feel a bit more comfortable on the range, or at a match, if they know what is expected. Originally I thought I was just lucky that 99% of the people at my gun club were nice and polite. After I finished dozens of interviews it became obvious that the lady shooters I spoke with think their club members are the best. Keep in mind that for a number of years I watched my daughters compete in other sports. The participants, and the spectators, at a number of these sports were not so nice. So for me the shooting sports were a refreshing environment after those experiences.

➤ If you're going to a pre-planned program, like "Women On Target," make sure you RSVP well in advance. Arrive at least 10 minutes early. The volunteers running this program appreciate being able to start on time and so do the other attendees. It's a great time to meet other new shooters and feel more comfortable in your new environment.

➤ If you attend a small club match I'd recommend arriving at least 30 minutes before the starting time. Most match directors like to do a tour, also called a walk-through, of each shooting area or stage. The walk-through is done prior to the actual start time of the match. This is also the time when new shooters are put on a squad with experienced participants. When you arrive a bit early it leaves you time to pay your match fees and still get on your equipment without having to hurry.

➤ As you get comfortable with local matches you start to move from being the "new shooter" to being a familiar face at the club. Start to participate (what I really mean is work) in the setup or teardown required to put on the match. The people at your club will appreciate anything and everything you do! Even though I am a princess I always make sure I do something for each match. Maybe I just staple paper targets onto the wood poles. Or at the end of the match I tear the paper targets off the shooting stands and throw them in the garbage. So in other words I do something to help.

➤ If you are attending a big match I'd suggest arriving at least one hour prior to the posted starting time. Quite often at a larger match you will be on a squad with people you might not know and you're in an unknown location. If you arrive at your first stage of the match late then you have missed your opportunity to ask questions. I used to tell the range officer right up front that I was an inexperienced shooter. I'm still not shy about asking questions if I'm not sure how a course is designed. For instance if there is window that needs to be opened so you can shoot through it, I'll ask them to show me how it works. Even after all these years I've never had anyone get upset with me for not understanding part of any shooting sport.

➤ When you get up to a competition you will notice that usually there are little time cards or score cards. These are the sheets used to record each person's accurate hits on the targets and/or time factor. After these cards are gathered up from all the members on your squad the RO will usually do a random drawing to see who goes first on each stage. If you are drawn first let them know you are a new shooter and a bit nervous. Don't demand not to go first, just make an honest request and I am confident it will be honored. This allows the new shooter the opportunity to observe the more experienced competitors in action before it is their turn.

➤ Regardless of the match size, find out where you are in the squad shooting order. Be aware of who is the competitor in front of you and behind you. I brought up earlier in the book that there is a right time and a wrong time to ask someone on your squad for help. If I'm shooting on a squad with a national champion, I find the best time to approach them might be right after the range officer has given the squad instructions. Or I'll ask them questions when I know they are not up in the next two positions. Keep in mind; these champions are usually professionally sponsored shooters. They take their shooting sport seriously and want to do the best they can on each stage. So if they seem a bit intense just before they run the event, it's understandable. I also don't ask them questions as soon as they are finished. I let them decompress a bit and then ask any questions I might have. Without exception these champions have been more then willing to help less experienced shooters.

➤ At any match, as I leave each stage I always make sure to thank the range officers in charge of that particular area. It's my way of telling these volunteers that I appreciate their time and effort, regardless of how I did on their stage. Over the years I have seen many of the same range officers. When you're polite to them it seems to come back to you three-fold when they see you again. One day you may go to a match where you may not know the other competitors. You may recognize some of the range officers and they are happy to assist you with whatever they can.

➤ The prize tables at big matches typically have contributions from different vendors within the firearms industry. Every time I leave a big match I make it a practice to email each sponsor from the match. On behalf of my husband and myself I thank them for their contributions. Remember, good manners don't cost money, though in this case it costs a bit of time. Over the years I've gotten numerous responses back from the sponsors thanking me for my email. They let me know they very much appreciate getting thank you notes from the shooters.

➤ You'll remember somewhere in the past the old phrase: "If you don't have anything nice to say then don't say anything at all." The same phrase applies at the gun range. I'm not talking about safety issues, which are always important to address right away. I'm talking about a class going on at the gun range and maybe you shoot a gun that doesn't seem to be to your liking. By all means put it down and try some other type of firearm. Make an effort not to announce to the whole group that this gun is "hard to shoot" or something along those lines. There are probably a number of other new lady shooters near you. While you may not like a particular type of gun it could work fine for them, unless now they're too apprehensive to even try it.

➤ This next manners issue is for all shooters, not just new shooters. Ever notice that if you are intensely supportive of one particular athletic team that someone else will be just as intensely against that team? Shooting sports aren't any different. We all have particular types of guns and events that we like and others that we don't like. The point I'm trying to make is that I think every shooting sport has its good points! Do yourself a favor and don't go into any one shooting sport and be negative about another shooting sport. Quite often negative comments come back to haunt you and possibly alienate a potential new club member. I am confident that the entire gun industry, including clubs, ranges and Second Amendment groups, can find some common ground. It stands to reason that all of these entities would like to see shooting sports in the United States continue to grow.

Lingo for Ladies...

We aren't going to discuss every type of gun. That's way too technical for me and I don't mind admitting it. This chapter relates to terms that seem common "lingo" for shooting sports or gun clubs across the United States. I think you'll agree that there are several terms in shooting that could be misconstrued. I'll give you a good example. About a year ago I mentioned to a new gal shooter at our club that she should bring more than one magazine with her for a local club match. The next weekend she brought out several older issues of Good Housekeeping. She placed them in the ladies restroom at the range. The reading material was nice but I was more interested in her bringing out more magazines for her gun.

Debbie Ferns participating at a local 3-gun match. She is using a 12-gauge shotgun, also called a "long gun."

The magazine I was referring to is a detachable tube, which is actually part of the gun that holds several bullets. (Some people refer to them as clips but more often they are called magazines.) Depending on the type of firearm a single magazine can typically hold six or more bullets for a pistol. A magazine for an AR-15 can hold 30 or more bullets. Pressing the trigger activates the magazine to give you one bullet at a time. (In some rifles you only load one bullet manually at a time, so there is no magazine.) A magazine is generally considered not to be disposable and is a term used most often for semi-automatic weapons. Some revolver shooters will call their ammunition holders "moon clips." So even in terms of magazines the "lingo" could continue on forever.

"Rifles, Handguns and Shotguns…Oh My!" – Thanks to Hollywood some people think that these guns shoot several bullets within a second and never run out of ammunition. You have been misled! Each of these firearms shoots one bullet at a time, every time the trigger is pressed. Rifles are used for longer distance shooting. Shotguns are used for closer targets and utilize a wide range of ammunition. Rifles and shotguns are sometimes referred to as long guns. When I talk about handguns that can take in everything from semi-automatic pistols to revolvers. Rifles, shotguns and hand-guns come in all sorts of makes, models, sizes and power levels or calibers.

"Ammo or Rounds"…These terms are commonly used on the range and refer to ammunition or bullets used in every type of gun. The bullets come in several different shapes and sizes to fit each type of gun.

"Caliber"…Refers to the size of the bullet, the diameter of the bullet. The bigger the caliber typically the bigger the hole the bullet will leave on the target.

"Range Officer"…I refer to them as RO while other sports call them umpires or referees. The RO usually refers to the person/persons in charge of one stage at your match.

"It's a cold range"…. That doesn't mean that you need a jacket in July at the Tucson range. This refers to the range rule indicating that it doesn't allow any loaded guns, except when you are at the line of fire. So don't drive up with any type of gun already loaded. All your gun gear should be in a bag in your vehicle. When you get to your match area ask the range officer or another participant where your gun bag should be placed. Then ask when the guns should be taken out of their bags. Assume that every range is a cold range.

"Going hot"…All people within hearing distance of that command should be prepared that a competitor is going to start shooting at a nearby range. This command is given to remind nearby spectators/competitors that ear and eye pro-tection needs to be in place. One new shooter, who was in her early 50's, started to laugh when she heard the RO give this command to me. She thought he was talking about my hot flashes, though I prefer to call them power surges.

"Clear your weapon"...When I heard this the first time at the indoor range I could have sworn the RO said: "Clean your weapon." I made sure the gun was empty and didn't have any bullets. Then I laid it on the shooting table facing downrange. I bent down to get a cleaning rag from my bag and started polishing my gun. Everyone was giving me a quizzical look and it dawned on me that no one else was cleaning his or her gun. Typically the command "clear your weapon" is a common one to make sure there are no bullets in your gun. At a match you will clear your gun before you put it back into your holster or back on a gun rack. Range attendants will use this command, and several others, so that people can safely go down-range to score or tape their targets.

There are several other descriptions that a new shooter will get to know as they spend more time at the range. I realize this is only a small sample of the "lingo" used and represents more of the shooting sports that I'm used to. If you aren't sure about a certain gun term I'd recommend asking the RO at your gun club. When you think about it, each sport has its own language; shooting sports isn't any different.

Resources

Amateur Trapshooting Association (ATA) – www.shootata.com

American Handgunner – www.sanjuanrange.com

BANG, Inc. (Kay Clark-Miculek & Jerry Miculek) – www.bang-inc.com

Ben Avery (BASFAZ) – www.basfaz.com

Bianchi Cup – www.nrahq.org/compete/nm – actionshooting.asp

Bowling Pins – www.pinshooters.homestead.com

Boy Scouts – www.mercerarea-bsa.org/shooting

Bullseye – www.bullseyepistol.com

Camp Perry – www.cpmr-oh.org

Civilian Marksmanship Program (CMP) – www.odcmp.com

Cowboy Mounted Shooting Association (CMSA) – www.cowboymountedshooting.com

Desert Creations (Jeanie Darnell – web designer) – www.desertcreations.com

DIVAS – www.txdiva.com

Brian Enos (awesome shooting web site!) – **www.brianenos.com**

Fifty Caliber Shooters Association (FSCA) –
www.fcsa.org

4-H Shooting Sports Foundation –
www.4-hshootingsports.org

Glock Shooting Sports Foundation (GSSF) –
www.gssfonline.com

Bill Goloski (Logo design) –
goloskidesign@hotmail.com

Julie Goloski –www.juliegoloski.com

Kim Gorham – www.brassbags.com

International Confederation Organization of Revolvers
(ICORE) – www.icore.org

International Defense Pistol Association (IDPA) –
www.idpa.com

International Handgun Metallic Silhouette Association
(IHMSA) – www.ihmsa.org

International Practical Shooting Confederation (IPSC) –
www.ipsc.org

Internet Shooting Directory – www.shootguns.info

International Steel Challenge Shooting Association
(SCSA) – www.steelchallenge.com

Ladies Skeet Classic – www.ladiescharityskeetclassic.org

Lady Smith & Wesson – www.bang-inc.com/
ladysmithinfo.htm

Masters Match – www.themasters.org

Rocky Meadows (SASS #18501) – Search Yahoo under Rocky Meadows

National Association of Shooting Ranges (NASR) – www.wheretoshoot.org and www.rangeinfo.org

National Association of Women Business Owner (NAWBO) – www.nawbo.org

National Muzzle Loading Rifle Association (NMLRA) – www.nmlra.org

National Rifle Association (NRA) - www.nra.org

National Shooting Sports Foundation (NSSF) – www.nssf.org

National Skeet Shooting Association (NSSA) – www.nssa-nsca.com

National Sporting Clays Association (NSCA) – www.nssa-nsca.com

NRA Whittington Center (NRAWC) – www.nrawc.org

Otero Practical Shooting Association – www.opshooter.org

Pima Pistol Club – www.pimapistol.org

Rio Salado Sportsmans Club – www.riosaladosportsmans.club

Robert Ian Productions – www.robertian.com

Rocky Mountain 3-gun – www.trm3g.homestead.com

Scottsdale Gun Club – www.ScottsdaleGunClub.com

Second Amendment Foundation (SAF) – www.saf.org

Second Amendment Sisters (SAS) – www.2asisters.net

Shopping For Mr. Right (Marsha Petrie Sue) – www.marshapetriesue.com

Single Action Shooters Society (SASS) – www.sassnet.com

Snipers Paradise Match – www.snipersparadise.com

South River Gun Club – www.southrivergunclub.com

Sportsmen Team Challenge Association (STC) – www.sportsmansteamchallenge.com

Steel Challenge Shooting Association (SCSA) – www.steelchallenge.com

Superstition Mountain Mystery 3-Gun (SMM3G) – www.smm3g.com

Robert Townsend (Townsend Photography) – rtown98@direcway.com

Tombstone Tactical Target Systems (Greg Stutz) – www.tombstonetactical.com

Tucson Rifle Club – www.tucsonrifleclub.org

United Special Sportsmen Alliance (USSA) – www.deerfood.com

United States Practical Shooting Association (USPSA) – www.uspsa.org

Videosyncrasy LLC (Bob Martin – Producer) – REMLTD@aol.com

Zia Rifle & Pistol Club – www.ziarifleandpistolclub.com

ORDER FORM

Order Online At:
www.BabesWithBullets.net

Mail To:
Bullseye Trading Post
7850 N. Silverbell Road
Suite 114-315
Tucson, Arizona 85743

Fax To:
520 572-1745

Sales tax: Please add 5.6% for products shipped to Arizona addresses.

Shipping: United States: $4 for the first book and $2 for each additional book. International: Based on ship-to location and current rates; please call for exact amounts. Shipping cost subject to postal rate changes.

Plese send me _____ copies of Babes With Bullets
at $15 each (plus shipping)

Total Amount of order (including shipping) _____

PLEASE PRINT

Name _____

Street Address _____

City/Province _____ State _____

Zip/Postal Code _____ Country _____ Phone _____

E-mail _____

☐ **VISA** ☐ **MasterCard** ☐ Check/Money Order

Card No. | | | | | | | | | | | | | | | | |

Exp. Date _____ Signature _____

Credit card orders will be processed under Bullseye Trading Post LLC